PRACTICAL GARDEN PROJECTS

GROUND FORCE

PRACTICAL GARDEN PROJECTS

Tommy Walsh

BBC

This book is published to accompany the television series entitled *Ground Force*, which was first broadcast in 1997. The series was produced by Bazal (part of GMG Endemol Entertainment) for BBC Television.

Executive Producer: Carol Haslam
Producer/director: John Thornicroft

Published by BBC Worldwide Limited, Woodlands, 80 Wood Lane, London W12 OTT

First published 2000

ISBN 0 563 55147 X

Commissioning Editor: Nicky Copeland
Project Editor: Rachel Brown
Designer: Isobel Gillan
Illustrator: Amanda Patton
Picture Researcher: Susannah Parker

Set in Fruitiger
Printed and bound in Great Britain by Butler & Tanner Ltd, Frome and London
Colour separations by Radstock Reproductions Ltd, Midsomer Norton
Cover printed by Belmont Press Ltd, Northampton

The soundtrack to the BBC TV series *Ground Force*, specially composed by Jim Parker and performed by the Black Dyke Band, is now available from all good retailers on the BBC Music label (catalogue number WMSF 6015–2).

Acknowledgements
With thanks to Chris Short, Susan Bell, Will Shanahan, Amanda Patton, Isobel Gillan and Rachel Brown.

Contents

Introduction

If you'd heard the word 'garden' ten years ago, probably the only things that would have come to mind were flowers, lawns and weeding. We seem to have come a long way in a very short time. Thanks to an explosion of books and television programmes in the recent past, people are increasingly coming to realize that the garden isn't just a plot of land in which to grow things. The modern garden has become an extension of the house, an architectural statement for some but certainly an 'outside room' for most of us.

Today DIY shops are laden with cheap tools and materials and the television screen is full of odd people sneaking around in other people's gardens while they're out… But that's another story.

I couldn't be happier about the way things are going. I've spent more years than I can remember busily renovating and redesigning people's gardens with new paths and patios, fabulous fences and timber features galore. I never tire of seeing how even a seemingly boring and uninspiring garden can be completely reborn with a little inspiration, a bit of planning and a lot of digging. And don't think that there's no point having big plans if you haven't got a big garden – more often than not, the smaller the garden is to begin with, the more dramatic the transformation when you're done.

I've tried to make this book do two things. First of all, I'd love you just to rummage through it, reliving some of those great *Ground Force* gardens, and generally getting enthused about the kind of changes you could make to your environment. It may be a simple arbour to complete that view from your kitchen window. It may be a new fence to keep the kids in, or the neighbours out, or it may be a complete revamp of that scabby patch of land right outside the back door. Sit back, flick through, and let your imagination take hold for a while.

Second, once your imagination finally hands over to determination and you actually get out of the chair and into the garden, I want you to use this book as a very practical and down-to-earth manual for some of the most common building methods used in landscape gardening. Let's face it, nothing you're going to do out there requires a lifetime's experience in engineering, but there are some very straightforward tips and techniques that are well worth knowing before you get stuck in. Many of them are to be found on the following pages.

Now obviously, in a book this size I can only touch upon the huge range of projects that might face you out there in the garden, but what I've tried to do is pick subjects that will teach you general rules and principles, which can then be applied to any number of projects of your own invention. For example, once you know how to build a brick wall and have mastered the carpentry of the lean-to pergola, it's not a huge leap from there to constructing a brick and timber shed, or even a greenhouse. So, if the exact project you need isn't in this book already, don't panic. Once you've read through it to the end, you'll be both confident and capable of turning your building skills in any direction you choose. It's your garden. The sooner you turn it into exactly what you want, the sooner everyone can get out there and start enjoying it.

BUILDER'S BASICS

The biggest mistake anyone can make when tackling the projects I've included in this book is to think: 'Everything will be fine, just so long as I finish it all off with some care and attention.' Wrong. The only way to guarantee that 'everything will be fine' with these types of construction is to start it all off with some care and attention. Good planning, good projects. It's as simple as that.

Now I'm not suggesting that you need a full-blown military campaign organized just to mow the lawn – all I'm saying is that you need to think through each and every stage of a project before you begin, not as you're going along. The time to discover that you need three more slabs to finish off the patio is while you're wandering through the shop, not when you're half-way into it and wading ankle-deep through wet concrete. It may sound obvious, but for any major task you need to start by thinking: Where will it be? How big will it be? What skills, tools and materials am I going to need to build it? How am I going to get all that stuff on to the site, and how am I going to get all the rubbish I create off again? How long will it all take? What weather do I need while I'm working? Do I need help? Do I need my head testing? Is there anyone nearby I could persuade to do it all for me instead?

With all this firmly in mind, I'm now going to let you in on the biggest secret in garden DIY. There are only two tools you'll ever need to ensure that every project comes out just as you'd imagined it and right on budget. Best of all, you can buy them both for the price of a packet of crisps and carry them around in your shirt pocket... All you need is something called 'a pencil', and something called 'a piece of paper'. That's it. Any good stationery shop should be able to point you in the right direction if you're not too familiar with the terms. Armed only with these two items you can plan, design, measure up, order up and accurately cost out everything in this book. Do that before you even begin to think about dusting off the shovel, and you will save yourself piles of superfluous materials and many hours of wasted time. So, you've been told, let the fun begin...

FAR LEFT: Regular checks along a builder's line will help ensure fences stay straight during construction.

LEFT: Transform your garden with a brightly coloured deck.

RIGHT: Once you've mastered the basics, experiment with your own ideas for innovative garden features.

HOW MUCH TO TACKLE?

This book is full of fun, practical and inspirational projects for you to select and apply to your own garden design. However, just before we launch headlong into a swirl of sawdust and cement, let me give you one word of caution. While it's very tempting to think that once you're armed with a jigsaw and a power drill there's no limit to what you can create in the garden, your ambitions must be tempered by a healthy dash of common sense and practicality. It's well known that Rome wasn't built in a day – it's less often remembered that very little of it was knocked up with a bit of timber and some rawlplugs.

There's no question that you can do some great things in the garden with some pretty rudimentary DIY skills and equipment, but always limit your projects to something that you have the time, the talent, the tools and, above all, the temperament to complete. Now I'm the last person in the world to stop you going out there and getting stuck into some serious carpentry or hard-landscaping, but if you're remotely unsure as to whether you have what it takes to complete the big projects, then start off with something on a somewhat smaller scale. The beauty of this book is that it shows you how to learn perfect construction techniques, not just particular projects. Once you have mastered the skills you need to erect a small stone wall, for example, there's actually nothing to stop you building one right around your garden if that's what you want. Similarly, the lean-to pergola we feature was built to span a small patio, but the method of construction I used holds true whether the distance you wish to cover is the length of a greenhouse or a manor house. Once you've grasped the basic principles of each different project, they can all be scaled up or down to suit the individual needs of your particular garden.

Raised beds are quick to build and make a stunning focal point.

Scheduling

You don't have to take on the whole of your garden, single-handed, in one afternoon. In exactly the same way that I suggest you plan each individual project in detail before you start, if you're looking to carry out a number of improvements all over your plot then treat the whole thing as one big project and order it accordingly. Work out everything you would like to alter in the garden, decide on how all those changes are going to interact with each other, and then set out some kind of schedule for the work involved. Just because your plans include a number of distinct projects, there's no need for each of them to be started and finished before you can begin anything anywhere else in the garden. Nobody wants to turn their garden into one huge building site, but you may well find that dovetailing together similar aspects of different projects will ultimately save you both time and money. For instance, it may be that several of your plans involve some substantial concrete foundations, in which case it would make sense to dig out all the trenches first and then choose one sunny weekend to hire in a concrete mixer and pour in all the concrete in one go. Similarly, you may well have two or three different types of timber construction in mind for various parts of the garden. So rather than running back and forth to the DIY shed for different lengths of wood, you could amalgamate all your requirements and put in one large order (with the possibility of attracting a discounted price) to the local timber yard, and have them deliver everything you need all at once. As long as you have somewhere convenient to store the wood, there's no reason why you shouldn't then spend the next few months building your timber structures at your leisure, confident in the knowledge that everything you need is already to hand.

The key principle

Garden DIY is meant to be fun. I do it all day every day, come rain or come more rain, and I still get a real kick out of seeing the finished landscapes come together.

A mortise joint (where a slot is cut in one piece of wood to accommodate another) adds strength to any timber construction.

For you, doing it as a hobby or for relaxation, it should be even more enjoyable. Above all, don't lose sight of that key principle. If what you're doing becomes a chore, or worse still a good old-fashioned nightmare, then something has gone terribly wrong. Take it from someone who is regularly asked to work minor miracles in just two days: the trick to keeping it enjoyable is to plan your work so that you don't take on more than you can comfortably achieve in the time you have available. Far better to break a large project down into smaller separate packages of work, and then tackle one each evening or weekend, than to find yourself out in the cold and decking by torchlight. Not only does this take the fun out of the project, you'll also end up tempted to cut corners and 'bodge' things just to get it all finished.

Also, don't forget that a large amount of the tedious and time-consuming aspects of garden construction can now be tackled by a neat little device called a telephone. This may be Do-It-Yourself, but let's not be silly about it.

If you really like the idea of getting to grips with a particular project, but there are certain aspects of it that you just don't have the time or the enthusiasm to tackle, then there's always someone you can call to come and sort it out for you. From a jobbing labourer to do some digging, right up to a specialist brickie to create a fancy bit of walling for you, you'd be surprised what you can find in the small ads of your local paper. Also on the end of the phone are a load of equipment hire companies, armed with seemingly everything from shovels to mechanical diggers. If you've got to do something boring or backbreaking, then the chances are someone may well have already come up with a machine that you can hire to do it faster and easier. Give your local hire shop a call, pick their brains a bit – and discover some of the little gadgets they have up their sleeves.

ORIENTATION

Although all the projects in this book are designed to be pretty straightforward to construct, don't be fooled into thinking that you're just messing about out there in the garden. You're not. This book will teach you how to tackle things that can make a huge and lasting effect on your garden, your house and the way in which you live there. With that ability comes the responsibility for planning out the location and orientation of your projects so that you don't end up building the right thing in the wrong place, the wrong thing in the right place or, most embarrassing of all, the wrong thing in the wrong place but still where everyone can see it! Getting this part of the process right is not rocket science, but it does require a moment's thought and contemplation. At a purely practical level, there are four key issues you need to consider when building anything outside: the light, the weather, access and view. Not all of those will apply to every project but, for something like a patio or summerhouse, all of them need considering.

This easy-to-build kit arbour is a perfect place to sit and relax.

Hard landscaping features are difficult to move. Think carefully about their position before you start building.

Light

This is the first and foremost consideration. The whole point of living outside is fresh air and sunshine, even if that sunshine may have to push its way through a few grey clouds every so often. If you're thinking of a nice little deck on which to sip your coffee of a morning, then obviously you want a clear view east. Alternatively, if you're more in the market for sundowners then you'll want a clear view of – well, the sun going down, I guess, which means (unless you're holding this book upside-down) facing west. During the rest of the day (assuming you live in the northern hemisphere) all your light's going to be coming from the south so, whichever way you look at it, building a north-facing patio is not a great idea. Alternatively, if you already have an area of the garden that faces towards the sun but you can't use it during the midday heat of summer, you might want to consider something like a lean-to pergola to give yourself some shade there. Finally, remember that unless you live on the equator, the sun will rise and set in a slightly different place on the horizon as the seasons change. Don't use any measurements or sightings that you make in the depth of winter as a foolproof blueprint for where the summer sun will appear.

Weather

This is rather less predictable than light, but just as important. Wherever you live, there will be a prevailing wind direction, and if you're out in the garden on a regular basis it won't take you long to work out what that is. Wind brings all sorts of things with it: warm air, cold air, strong destructive gusts, the smoke from next-door's barbecue and, of course, that strange smell from number 37 that everyone has been too polite to mention… However, probably the worst thing that wind brings with it is rain and damp when the weather gets bad. Whatever you're building in the garden, whether it's for you to enjoy or just for the plants, you need to be conscious of where the nice warm breezes are going to come from as well as the foul wet ones. The more protected your outdoor leisure areas are, the more use you will get out of them as the years go by, and always remember that any aspect of your construction that is exposed to the worst of the weather will need both protection and regular maintenance.

Access

Not so often considered, but this is still very important. Obviously, no one is going to build something in the garden that's impossible to get to (unless it's a cesspit!), but how people get to your masterpieces is crucial. You have to remember that most of us are lazy. The shortest route between two points is always a straight line, so your long and ornate winding path may prove completely pointless when the kids just run across the lawn to get to their new playhouse. Whatever you're building, consider how people will be most likely to get there, which directions they'll move around in once they're there, and where they'll want to go when they leave. Straight paths

between different areas of your garden can be pretty boring (and a winding approach always has far more potential drama about it), but they're the routes most people will take unless you use either planting or some kind of constructed feature to actively force them along the path you want them to follow. Rather more mundane, but just as important, is access to and from the house. If you want a garden area in which to eat and entertain a great deal, building it a long way from the kitchen is not always a great idea. You may well think you can do all the cooking on a barbecue and so save yourself having to make frequent trips into the house, but where are all those lovely salads going to come from and, more importantly, how cold is that beer going to stay on its long journey from the fridge? A little forethought before you begin to build will reap its rewards many times over once the job's done right.

The view

There are two ways of looking at this, if you see what I mean. Not only will everything you build in the garden become part of the actual landscape, and therefore need to complement what's already there, but it will often be a location from which you settle down to view the world around you. In short, one man's view is another man's viewpoint. As far as 'the view' is concerned, features that you intend to be purely decorative – a feature wall or a plant climber, for example – need to be carefully placed into the environment so that they fit in well with the existing garden. The materials you employ need to be sympathetic to their surroundings, and the overall scale of the project needs to balance with other features around it. Think of your garden as a picture, but one that can be viewed from many different angles. Sometimes you'll be building structures that form an attractive part of that picture – some steps maybe, or a window box – at other times you will be constructing a frame through which the picture can be viewed, some fencing perhaps or a pergola by the house. However, sometimes you will be building 'the viewpoint', possibly a little seat in an arbour or a massive high-level deck. You must be conscious of which way people will want to look, and try to position your viewpoint so that they have the most interesting vista of the garden to enjoy.

PLANNING

At the risk of getting boring, planning your job correctly is the most important stage of the whole process. To do this properly you will first need an accurate map of the site on which you intend to work. If this site happens to

Be imaginative with your garden design. Curved paths and hidden corners are much more attractive than straight paths and stark features.

your first point (point A) will be. Plot the scaled-down distance between point A and point B and mark a dot where point B will be. The location of these points on the paper is not so important, but they must be exactly the right distance apart. From these first two marks you will eventually create a plan of the entire area. If, for example, you were mapping out for a patio at the back of the house and points A and B were the corners of the house, it would make sense to place those two points at the top of your paper and then work down from there.

Now, 'here comes the science'. For every subsequent feature you now wish to mark on your plan, be it a tree or the corner of a lawn, all you have to do is pop into the garden and measure how far away it is from both points A and B. Then, go back to your plan, set a pair of compasses

Your triangulation diagram should look something like this.

If sunshine is important to you, make sure you build your deck where it shines for the maximum amount of time each day.

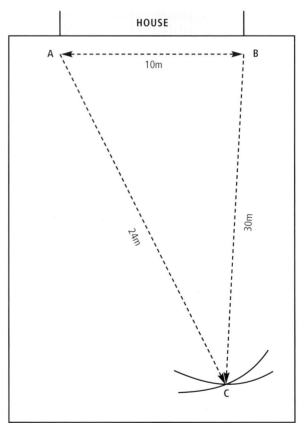

be a nice neat square of perfectly flat, empty land then your task is pretty easy. If, however, it is more like every garden I seem to end up working in, then it will be a misshapen jigsaw of borders, bushes and old brickwork all set on strangely undulating slopes and decorated with stinging nettles. In cases like this the only hope for an accurate scale drawing is what's called 'triangulation'. Sounds like a badge you might get in the Boy Scouts, but it's actually dead easy and dead useful.

Triangulation

Pick two fixed reference points which are spread a fair distance apart across your plot of land. Either end of the house wall is a good example, or two big trees. Think of these as points A and B and use a tape measure to establish the distance between them. Moving on to your drawn plan, decide on the scale at which you will be working and mark a cross on the page roughly where

to the distance between the feature you wish to locate and point A, stick the spike in point A and then draw a small arc on the plan roughly where the new feature should be. The less confident you are about guessing where this will be, then the longer your arc. Do the same for the distance between point B and the new feature, and draw another arc out from point B to where the feature should be. Where these two arcs cross is the exact location of point C. You now have a wonderfully simple system with which to calculate the position of all the boundaries and features that constitute the entire site. Every position that you need to mark down can be measured off from your two original triangulation points, or indeed from any other two points you have already marked on the plan. Once you have joined all these points with any straight lines that run between them (the edge of a lawn for example) and completed your map of the site 'as is', you can then use tracing paper to mark out where your new hard-landscaping or timber constructions will sit. It is, of course, just as important to get the dimensions of your new additions as accurate as the existing landscape, for this plan is your key to specifying the exact type and quantity of materials you will need to complete the project in hand.

QUANTIFYING

There is only one surefire way of coming home from the DIY shed without having bought too many or too few materials for the job in hand: you have to know exactly how much you'll need before you go. If you end up wandering round the shelves with a 'back-of-an-envelope' sketch in one hand and a credit card in the other you're certain to come unstuck. Either you'll find two-thirds of the way through a crucial stage of construction that you've run out of something vital, or you'll complete the job only to find that you still have a pile of unused and expensive stuff that is difficult enough just to shift, let alone get rid of. Quantifying means using your ground plan to calculate the different types and amounts of materials necessary to complete

the whole job or the next stage of construction. Given your new-found skills with both scale drawing and triangulation, we will assume that you're now in possession of a plan that is both accurate enough and detailed enough to provide exact measurements for every dimension of the structure, including any foundations that might be necessary. Starting from the bottom up (which is always best when building, I find), let's look at what you're going to need to bury below ground first.

Foundations

These are the unsung hero of every major building project. Once it's complete you never notice them but, if you've not put them in properly, they will soon make their lack of

Even though timber grows on trees, make sure you buy as much as you need.

presence felt. (Just ask anyone who's had to have their house underpinned.) Calculating the materials needed for decent foundations under a wall or a patio is pretty straightforward. Each project will specify the mixture of cement and ballast that you require (usually 6 parts ballast to 1 part cement) and the 'volume calculator' on these pages will show what quantity of materials you need. So, for example, let's say you're going to pour a slab of foundation which needs to be 1 metre by 4 metres, and the project instructions specify that it needs to be 25cm deep: 4 x 1 is 4, so that's 4 square metres multiplied by 0.25 metres depth – giving you a total volume for the foundations of 1 cubic metre. (If you're working in old money, say your slab is 3ft by 9ft and 1ft deep: that gives you 27 cubic feet, or exactly 1 cubic yard.) Now you'll probably be buying your cement and ballast from the DIY shed in individual 'bags', which are all a standard size now. There are about fifty 'bags' of material to each cubic metre (or yard – to be honest there's not a lot of difference), and if you're working at the standard 6:1 mix that means you'll need to divide fifty by seven, which is about seven, and then use that figure to multiply up by one for the cement and by seven for the ballast. It's not an exact science, but you can use it to work out that you'll need about seven bags of cement and about forty-three bags of ballast to make up your total of fifty bags for the foundations.

It also sounds like you're going to need a month off work, a cement mixer and the shoulders of Arnold Schwarzenegger, but that's another story…

Always remember: if you're ordering materials in significant amounts it's often better to miss out the DIY sheds and find yourself a local builder's merchant instead. There you can order up sand and ballast by the cubic yard and bricks by the pallet load. Most of the decent merchants will then deliver right to your door in big 'dumpy bags'. One word of caution, though: 'right to your door' is just an expression, OK? You're going to have to organize somewhere far more convenient to store

'Volume calculator' METRIC

Depth/Area	1 sq m	5 sq m	10 sq m	50 sq m
7.5cm deep	0.08 cubic m, or about 4 bags	0.4 cubic m, or about 20 bags	0.75 cubic m, or about 40 bags	3.75 cubic m, or about 200 bags
15cm deep	0.15 cubic m, or about 8 bags	0.75 cubic m, or about 40 bags	1.5 cubic m, or about 80 bags	7.5 cubic m, or about 400 bags
30cm deep	0.3 cubic m, or about 16 bags	1.5 cubic m, or about 80 bags	3 cubic m, or about 160 bags	15 cubic m, or about 800 bags

'Volume calculator' IMPERIAL

Depth/Area	1 sq yard	5 sq yards	10 sq yards	50 sq yards
3in deep	0.08 cubic yard, or about 4 bags	0.4 cubic yard, or about 20 bags	0.8 cubic yard, or about 40 bags	4 cubic yards, or about 200 bags
6in deep	0.16 cubic yard, or about 8 bags	0.8 cubic yard, or about 40 bags	1.65 cubic yards, or about 80 bags	8 cubic yards, or about 400 bags
12in deep	0.33 cubic yard, or about 16 bags	1.65 cubic yards, or about 80 bags	3.3 cubic yards, or about 160 bags	16 cubic yards, or about 800 bags

these materials as they take up a lot of room. Ideally, try to get the delivery driver to hoist the dumpy bags into a space close to where you'll be building – it will save many tedious wheelbarrow journeys later on.

Quantifying your materials for other types of building project is just as easy, and there are a number of simple 'rules of thumb' to help you out along the way.

Patios and paths

You're looking at four standard 500mm slabs per square metre (or four standard 18in slabs per square yard).

Crazy paving, however, is made up from slabs or stones of all different shapes and sizes – to order that up correctly you'll need a calculator and a good psychiatrist. It's not called crazy paving for nothing. Your best bet is to ask the supplier how much a ton of the stuff will cover and then work it out from there. It should give you about 10 square metres (12 square yards) – but at least if it all goes wrong you've got someone else to blame.

Brick walls

For normal ones, you should allow about fifty bricks per square metre/yard, twice that if you're building a double-thickness (23cm/9in) wall. At the standard 6:1 mix for the mortar when bricklaying, six bags of soft sand and one bag of cement will bed in about 200 bricks, or 4 square metres (about 4½ square yards) of single-thickness (10cm/4in) wall. When building stone walls and ordering material by weight, you can assume 1 ton of rough stone will give you about 8–10 square metres (9½–12 square yards) of single-thickness wall. But different types of stone weigh different amounts, so this is not 'set in stone'.

Decks

There is no easy way of giving you general rules, I'm afraid. Once you have an accurate plan of your deck, you'll have to pick your way through the drawing, adding up all the lengths of different-sized timber and making an educated guess at bolts, screws and the like.

TOOLS AND MATERIALS

All the planning and preparation in the world isn't going to get you anywhere unless you have the right tools and materials to turn to. Here's a handy checklist that should see you through any of the projects I'm suggesting here.

Tools

There are a fair few different tools mentioned in the course of this book. Some of them you're almost sure to have already, while some of them you may need to buy or hire in. The golden rule when buying any new tool is always go for the best one you can sensibly afford. There will always be cheaper alternatives available and there will always be very good reasons why those alternatives are cheaper in the first place. Unfortunately these are reasons that don't usually become apparent until you've got the tool home and started to use it.

I won't bore you here with a list of every tool you might ever need, but I will mention a few items that are worth investing in if you don't already have them.

A cordless drill/driver Without doubt the single most pleasurable and important thing you will ever have with you in the garden, unless you've got children. Even then, it's often a close-run thing. After all, how many kids do you know that can drill holes through wood, masonry and metal then pop in another fitting and drive home all manner of fixings from screws to bolts? All without any moaning and all without any need to be wired to the mains by way of encouragement. A well-made, powerful drill/driver will help you fly through most of the projects in this book and ensure that whatever you want to drill or fix is dispatched quickly and efficiently.

A DIY essential, the spirit level is fundamental for many projects.

There are many types of product on the market, but ideally the one you want has at least a 12v motor, though 14v is better and 18v is fantastic. Basically, the more powerful the motor the harder the material you can drill though. If you're planning to drill into masonry on a regular basis then get a drill/driver that has something called 'hammer action'. This doesn't mean you can spin the thing around and use the handle to knock in nails – it's a little switch that will vibrate the drill as it spins and punch into the hardest of concrete and stone. Also, if you're going to use the thing as your main screwdriver (and even if you don't think you are, believe me you will) then consider a drill/driver that has a torque control. This nifty little collar around the chuck allows you to set the screwdriver bit so that it will spin freely as soon as the screw has been driven firmly home – but just before you rip out all the slots on the head so that you can never get the screw out again! Finally, twin speed is nice, slow for screwdriving and fast for drilling, but not really essential. Cordless is definitely nice, but if it's a choice between a very low-powered cordless or a mains-driven unit then I'd be tempted to go for the more powerful corded one and invest in an extension lead for good measure.

Drill bits There are different drill bits for different materials, and using the wrong one will quickly ruin whichever one is fitted into the drill at the time. Some manufacturers now make drill bits that will tackle wood and metal, but masonry always requires a drill bit all of its own. Get yourself a small set of whichever type you need, so that you always have the right size (diameter) of drill bit to hand.

An expanding rule 'Measure twice, cut once' they say, but no one ever mentions that you need to measure with something accurate and robust. A good metal rule, ideally about 5 metres (16ft) long, will never shrink or stretch and always give you reliable measurements. It's

Power drivers are great for saving you time and energy.

best to get one with some kind of lock on the casing so that you don't lose any fingers when the rule snaps back in unexpectedly.

A spirit level Make sure that the spirit level you buy has got at least two bubble tubes – one to tell you when it's horizontal and another to tell you when it's vertical (or 'plumb' as we call it). You can buy spirit levels over a metre in length, but I'd recommend buying a shorter one. If it's not long enough for the job in hand you can always place it on to a long straight wooden batten, but make sure the batten really is straight, otherwise all the levelling in the world isn't going to save you…

A crosscut handsaw Yes, I know there are things called jigsaws and circular saws on sale nowadays, but they aren't always what you need. A decent 'crosscut' handsaw (one that's designed to cut across the grain of the wood, for shortening planks and the like) will always come in useful

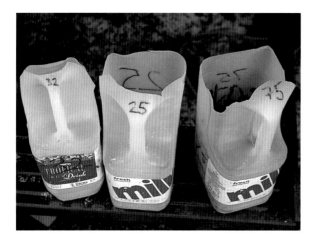

Empty plastic milk containers make perfect holders for screws and nails.

whenever there's timber to be cut. Look for one that has the handle fitted at exactly 90 degrees to the blade, so that you can use it to mark right-angle cuts on your wood. Also, keep it clean when you're not using it so that it's always nice and sharp when you do. A quick wipe over with an oily cloth should do it, each time you put the saw away.

A tenon saw This little fellow is a short handsaw with a strong metal brace along its spine to keep the blade straight. It's meant for making small, accurate cuts in wood, such as for a mortise and tenon joint. It's happy to cut with the grain or across the grain of the timber, but if you let it get dirty and blunt then it won't be very happy no matter what you point it at.

A chisel The chisel did not become obsolete soon after they finished building the Ark. It is still an invaluable tool for timber craftsmen everywhere, and that includes you. If you're going to attempt anything like a mortise and tenon joint in your carpentry, then you'll need a nice sharp chisel to complete the task. And I do mean sharp: blunt chisels are worse than useless. It's probably best to buy them in a small set of three or four chisels to make sure you have the right size for the right job.

A bradawl One tiny tool, a thousand different uses. A bradawl is not what you'd describe as being at the 'high-tech' end of the tool market – it's really just a little spike with a handle. However, you'll be amazed at how useful that can be. A bradawl is great for marking screw points in wood, and will even make a little pilot hole for you (see Fixings, opposite) if you're putting small screws into softwood. A bradawl will also come in handy to scratch marks across wood where you're going to saw, especially when you've lost your third pencil that day.

Cramps Now there are some who believe that if God had meant us to indulge in DIY he would have given us more hands, but I think the creation of the cramp was his way of apologizing. Cramps are just hand-tightened devices for holding things firm on a temporary basis. They are dead useful for gripping wood while it glues, or just holding a brace to a post while you get it upright. There are now some really nifty 'quick-grip' versions on the market that you can practically operate single-handed.

Mole grips Not a method of pest control but more of a cross between large pliers and a small cramp. Mole grips can be adjusted to grasp any object from a tiny nailhead to a large nut, right up to a couple of wooden battens, and will then lock into place for as long as you need to hold on. Combined with an adjustable spanner, they make a pretty useful team around the garden.

Electric sanders If you want to finish off woodwork properly, for painting, or varnishing, or just for walking over, then there's no substitute for some vigorous and protracted sanding. Now unless the wood you're working on is no bigger than a shoebox, you will quickly discover that sanding by hand is one of the most tedious and exhausting hobbies known to man. If there's a lot of surface to be smoothed then get yourself an electric sander and a selection of sandpaper grades to use with it. Sandpaper comes in all guises from very coarse to very fine.

The rough stuff is for getting through the wood quickly while the smoother grades are for fine finishing work.

If you're looking to take off a significant amount of wood from the timber in question then you might want to consider an electric planer instead. This uses a spinning blade rather than paper, but it can dig down surprisingly quickly so be careful how long you use it for – and don't even bother plugging it in unless you're pretty confident with power tools already.

Powersaws Jigsaws are very popular and very useful in the garden – there are even some cordless versions starting to appear now. However, as with drills, you need to be sure you have selected the right fitting for the material you're working with. There are jigsaw blades for hardwood, softwood, metal and even ceramics. It's all written on the packet when you buy them, but once you've lost that packet and have nothing but a writhing mass of unmarked blades in the bottom of your toolbox the best tip to remember is: 'The bigger the teeth on the blade, the softer the material it is intended for.'

If you're planning to do some major cutting work, building a large deck for instance, you might want to look at an electric circular saw. Unlike the jigsaw, a circular saw will only make straight cuts through wood, but it will do so like the proverbial knife through butter. Again, the blades are interchangeable, so make sure you have the right one fitted for the material you're cutting. For my money, though, you're probably still better off, and certainly a lot safer, with a good old handsaw instead.

Bricklayer's trowel An invaluable tool, the bricklayer's trowel can scoop, level and even cut bricks in half. A proper bricklayer's trowel is an elongated diamond shape with one edge straight and the other slightly curved. The ones you'll find in the DIY shop are more likely to be straight on both sides, but are perfectly good enough for all the jobs in this book. The sharp end of the trowel is used for pointing between bricks, once they've been laid.

Fixings There's a dizzying selection of nails and screws on the shelves of every DIY shed. Ignore them. All you need is a load of dry lining screws, in various sizes, and you're ready for anything this book has to throw at you. These screws are actually meant for putting up plasterboard inside the house, but they will cope with all manner of more exciting projects than that. They are cross-head, so make sure you have suitable screwdrivers to fit, and the right attachments for your cordless drill/driver.

The trick to putting screws into wood so that they go exactly where you want them, is to drill little pilot holes first. The pilot hole will give the screw an easy start into the wood and then ensure that it continues its journey in

When building walls or patios, remember that too much mortar is preferable to too little. You can scrape off the excess later on.

exactly the direction you want. As for nails, I'd avoid using them wherever you can – they can't touch screws for strength and durability. But if you're intent on hammering down your deck then get hold of 'ring nails', which have little ridges all the way down to stop them coming out once they're in.

Garden tools You may well have all the forks and shovels you need around the garden, but if you're looking to get some new ones then remember this book is for people who want to do some proper building work, not a quiet afternoon's weeding. Get yourself some tools that are up to the task and make sure you have a nice broad shovel for loading sand and the like in and out of wheelbarrows.

Hiring It's all too easy to get seduced by the enormous range and ingenuity of the tools market and end up with a very extensive/expensive collection of kit that hardly ever sees the light of day. In reality, if you pick your tools carefully, there are only a handful of bits and pieces you really need to own outright. There are plenty of hire shops

out there now that will cater for all your hardware needs without you paying for anything more than a day's usage. Clearly, there's little point hiring in things like chisels or hammers, and I can't believe that anyone wouldn't get enough use out of a power drill/driver to make that a very good purchase, but there are numerous other items that might be worth hiring on a more casual basis.

For instance, that gorgeous new deck you're planning may well cry out for a circular saw to cut through the boards, but what are you going to do with it once the last screw's gone in? Bacon slicer? Frisbee? Only you can judge how much use you're likely to get from one particular tool but, if there's any danger of it being a one-day wonder, then hire it in. You can always buy one later if you find you can't bear to be parted from it. Conversely, let's say you've got a big patio to lay and some substantial paving to put down. That could mean a lot of foundation work, all of which would be far easier with a little concrete mixer on your side. Think about buying one for the weeks you need it, and then selling it on second-hand once you're done. It may add up a lot cheaper than hiring one all summer.

There are a multitude of tools that you can hire to make your life easier. This chop saw cuts lengths of timber in a fraction of the time it would take to do it by hand.

Materials

Check out the rest of this book and you'll soon come to realize there's a whole range of garden projects clamouring to lure you out of that comfortable armchair. The good news is most of them can be constructed with just a few simple materials. In fact, once you have a good knowledge of working with timber and cement, there's very little you can't tackle successfully.

Timber If you don't like working with wood, you might as well stop reading this book now. I love wood. Wood is an amazing material. You can play around with it like a kid's building toy, creating anything from a tiny matchbox to a massive cathedral, and yet once you leave it alone it will withstand years of strain and abuse. And it grows on trees!

Wood comes in two types, hard and soft. Hardwood is a heavy, close-grained material that will last outdoors for years on end. However, it comes from very slow-growing trees such as oak and mahogany, and is significantly more expensive than a softwood equivalent. Softwood comes from fast-growing deciduous trees such as pine and fir. It's pretty cheap, it's very easy to work with and it's light enough to carry around without a paramedic in attendance. Treated with the right substances – or 'tanalized' as it is known – softwood will last for decades out in the garden, even if it's buried in the soil. Every project in this book, even the decks, are made using only softwood. You can now get hardwoods from sustained forests without contributing to any great ecological disaster, but unless you're very confident about your carpentry skills you might just be wasting your money for no real return.

When buying your timber, check it for splits or large knotholes, which will be a real pain when you want to build with it. Also, a lot of the DIY sheds get the softwood out of the soil and into the stores so quickly nowadays that it's still dripping sap in your car on the way home. Softwood needs to dry out thoroughly before it can be worked with, and if that isn't done in a

If you're having materials delivered make sure they are left close to where you're working. You don't want to carry them too far.

controlled environment the planks will start to warp and twist. You can easily spot this in the shop by running your eye along the length of the timber from one end. If it's meant to be straight and it ain't, don't buy it.

When you buy timber you will quickly notice that the sizes quoted on the labels very often don't match the actual dimensions of the wood. This is not some global conspiracy, but merely the result of timber being sold in two different guises, 'sawn' and 'planed'. 'Sawn' planks are just as they come from the timber yard. The outside surfaces will be rough to the touch, but the sizes quoted on the label will actually match the size of the stuff you're buying. Far more popular nowadays is the 'planed' timber. This is the same stuff with about 3mm (⅛in) of surface taken off all the way around. It's smooth to the touch and pretty much ready to paint, but always comes out slightly smaller than the dimensions on the label.

Whatever type of timber you buy, the crucial thing is that it has been treated to withstand life outdoors without rotting. The most effective way of doing this is by 'pressure treating' the timber at source with a tanalizing process. Pressure-treated timber has a preservative forced right into the very heart of the wood that will stop it rotting in the garden – how far through the wood this stuff goes has a direct bearing on how well protected your construction will be. You can see how effective the tanalizing process has been by looking at a sawn end of the wood. If the dark coloration goes well into the middle of the plank it has been adequately protected, but if there's just a pathetic little rim of colour around the outer surface then you might as well build your project out of cardboard. You can get timber preservative and paint it on the wood yourself, but it will only really get a few millimetres into the timber. It's best kept just for touching up planks where you have sawn through to reveal untanalized areas in the heart of the timber.

Concrete and mortar Cement is the other material you're going to find under your fingernails from now on. Cement is the common ingredient that makes up both 'concrete' and 'mortar'. Combine cement with aggregate, ballast or sharp sand, add some water and you have concrete – the star of paths, hardstandings and foundations. Combine it with soft sand, add some water and you have mortar – the stuff that holds all the bricks together in your walls. The ingredients for both these tasty dishes are readily available at all the DIY sheds and builders' merchants, along with little extras like plasticizer and retardant to keep the stuff more workable for longer periods.

You can either mix up what you need on site (by hand or with a portable cement mixer) or you can even have the stuff delivered ready mixed – but you'd better have everything ready for it when it arrives. One cubic metre of concrete will take about thirty wheelbarrow loads to shift, and it's drying all the time…

If you're mixing mortar by hand – or rather, by shovel – measure out your sand or ballast first then add the cement and mix everything dry until you have an even-coloured pile. Make a little crater in the top and slowly add water, mixing all the time, until you have the consistency you need. If you're mixing in a machine, you'll need to add a little water straight away to keep everything moving smoothly. The usual formula for concrete and mortar is 6 parts sand or ballast to 1 part cement, but you may need to top up the cement content where you need additional strength. Finally, even though concrete looks to have become solid after just a few hours, it will take at least overnight in summer and two days in winter for the surface to be load-bearing. Even then, the chemical reactions that occur in setting concrete don't finally settle down for nearly a month after it's laid, at which point it will have achieved full strength.

For setting fence posts, you can now get a ready-to-use powder that's poured dry into your post hole and then packed down around the post itself. Holding everything where you want it to stay, you then add water to the mix which makes it set rock hard in just a few minutes. Probably not as strong as concrete, but significantly easier for small jobs – you might well want to keep a couple of bags knocking about for emergencies.

PREPARING THE SITE

OK, we know what we're doing, we've got the right tools and materials to do it with – all we need now is a nice clear spot to do it in… Sometimes, preparing the site might just involve shouting at the dog, at other times there may be quite a lot of natural and man-made obstacles in your path.

Trees

These can be a real nightmare, and if they're anything over 5–6 metres (20–25ft) high I wouldn't even bother trying to fell them. Get on the phone, get in a tree surgeon and put your feet up. Smaller trees can be tackled fairly easily, though. Start from the highest branches you can reach with a ladder and use a bow saw to cut off all the branches. Once that's done, cut through the trunk itself to leave a portion of the tree about 3 metres (10ft) high still standing. Now get a shovel and dig a hole around the base of the tree until you're about 60cm (2ft) away from the trunk all the way around. Use a 'felling axe' to cut through all the roots you can find and scrabble about to see if there are any more just below the soil. When you've cut through everything you can find down there, tie a rope to the top of the remaining trunk and pull. You may need to chop through some more roots as they become exposed, but hopefully the length of the trunk will give you enough leverage to get the thing down on to the ground. Once

The trick is not to cut off the branch you're standing on.

felled, saw the trunk up into manageable logs for burning or selling. If it's just a branch you're looking to remove, then cut all the smaller branches off it first to reduce the size and the weight when it falls. If it's a particularly big branch, start from one end and take it down in a series of cuts. Obviously, if the end you start from is the end where it joins the trunk this will be somewhat tricky!

Walls and buildings

Brick walls and old bits of building can usually be despatched with a well-aimed sledgehammer. However, with old garden walls, you may find the bricks will actually come out whole. (Try a little tap from a hammer to persuade them.) If they do, then it's worth spending the extra time salvaging them. The chances are they'll match the original bricks in your house and could prove very useful for some later building project of your own.

POWER AND SAFETY

You don't have two arms, two legs and two eyes so that it doesn't matter so much when you lose one. Safety in the garden is pretty much common sense, but unfortunately none of the tools you're using will have any at all. Every tool that can do you any serious damage will have information on how to use it correctly and safely. Read these instructions before you use the tool, not after and definitely not during. If the manufacturer recommends wearing safety equipment of any kind, that is probably because someone has already done something stupid and brought the potential danger to everyone's attention.

If you're using any tool that is going to start sending material flying through the air, then get some goggles over your eyes. Only Superman moves faster than a speeding bullet, and even he never messes with circular saws, masonry drills and the like.

Safety goggles are essential when materials may splinter or chip.

Tools that are sharp are made that way so that they will cut into anything and everything they come in contact with – make sure that isn't you. Ironically, sharp tools are probably more dangerous when you let them get blunt; it's then that they will tend to slip and seek out your unsuspecting fingers.

Corded power tools have a large whack of electricity running up the cable towards them. If you cut through that cable there is every chance you will become part of the ring main in your house. Whenever you use power tools outside, always make sure they are connected to the mains by what's called a residual current device (RCD): this little box will shut down the power as soon as it detects any disruption in the current, like you cutting through the cable with your jigsaw.

If you plan to have power out in the garden permanently, for exterior sockets perhaps or outdoor lighting, you must either get a qualified contractor to install a 240v system buried in proper protective conduits with weatherproof socket and switches, or just use one of the low-voltage lighting kits that are now available in every garden centre and DIY shed. If you have kids or burrowing pets, there is no substitute for the safety and peace of mind that a low-voltage system will offer.

Finally, by far the most dangerous item you will ever see loose in your garden is called a child. These small creatures are programmed from birth to seek out sharp objects and high places. What they can't put their fingers into they will try to put in their mouths and, when they can't do that, they will try to crawl under it or jump off it. Be warned, they have the agility and curiosity of small apes, combined with all the common sense of a particularly stupid lemming. On no account should you allow one of these creatures to wander unsupervised around your working environment, especially when 'clearing up your tools neatly' is not your strong suit. By all means get them involved in the construction process, but make sure it's with something that won't harm them.

Power tools are great labour-saving devices, but always refer to the manufacturer's instructions before you use them.

TRADE TALK

builder's line	a string stretched taut between two pins and used as a guide to keep brickwork level.	**goes off**	the hardening process for concrete. It takes weeks to complete fully, but the concrete is hard enough to work on in a couple of days.
jointing iron	a curved piece of metal shaped to smooth off mortar between courses of brick.	**mortise and tenon joint**	a method of strengthening timber joints. The end of one piece of wood is cut into a square peg, the 'tenon', which then fits snugly into a matching slot in the other, the 'mortise'.
offering up	placing material in the position where it will be secured. Done to mark in measurements or to fix into place.	**shuttering**	planks secured in place with pegs hammered into the ground. Used to make a shape into which concrete is poured. Once everything is dry the shuttering can be removed.
plasticizer	an additive that is put into mortar when it's mixed which makes it smoother to work with and more frost resistant.	**aggregate**	the stuff you mix with cement powder to make mortar or concrete. Ballast is a mix of sand and gravel and can be combined with cement powder to create smooth concrete.

BORDERS
and EDGES

The borders of your garden aren't just the place where your bit ends and someone else's land begins – how you choose to define and decorate those perimeters will have a major effect on the whole look of your outdoor environment. So before you go rushing off sinking post holes right across the croquet lawn, just remember the first rule of any boundary construction project: 'Work out why it's there, before you build it.' Sounds odd, I know, but this is the easiest – and possibly the most costly – advice to ignore. Fencing or garden screening can fulfil many different tasks. You might well want to provide a secure boundary around your property, but it's just as likely you'll need to plan projects that are designed to create a 'hidden garden', or hide away the compost heap, or define the border between lawn and flower bed. All different tasks, all requiring a different approach, with potentially very different materials.

LEFT: Use trelllis fences for breaking up boring garden spaces.

RIGHT: Natural stone walls are an attractive alternative to the traditional brick. Choose local stone for the best effect.

So, before you pick up that fence post, pick up a pencil and decide exactly what you need your fencing or walling project to achieve. Are you blocking out traffic noise, for example, or providing shelter from a particularly prevalent breeze? Do you want something that dramatically stands out from its surroundings, or subtly blends in? Then, when you have decided upon the job (or even jobs) your creation needs to perform, start working out the materials and design that will suit you best. Just so long as you always design and build with the primary purpose in mind, you can't go wrong. Honest.

In this section of the book I'm going to take you through some great 'starter projects', each designed to get you cracking and get you confident with the basic principles involved. After that, you can take your new-found skills and turn them to ever

more elaborate and more individual projects of your own design. I'm sure it won't be long before you come to realize that your borders and edges are some of the most eye-catching and effective methods of improving both the look and the value of your property.

Of course, the great thing about any walling, gate or fencing project is that there are now thousands of different designer gadgets and products readily available to you from the nearest garden centre or DIY shed. Better still, even when you've exhausted all those ready-made options, a few simple tools and some plain old lengths of timber will open up an infinite range of alternatives, each as unique and ingenious as your own imagination. Your border constructions can be anything from massive, bold architectural statements to the most delicate and stylish solutions.

Planning ahead

The first thing to consider when fencing is what effect your plans will have on other people. If you're building a fence along a boundary where your land meets your neighbour's, this consideration has legal implications. Local planning regulations usually allow you to put up a fence about 2 metres (6ft) high around your property. However, this will be affected by factors such as the proximity of your new fence to the public road, the type of construction you are planning to erect and which part of your neighbour's house lies directly behind the fence. Local by-laws are usually pretty sympathetic to anyone trying to improve the look or security of their property, but it's always worth checking the details with the council planning office before you make an expensive mistake.

Even where there are no legal considerations to your new boundary construction, it's a matter of courtesy to string a line down the intended route of your new fence and check that your neighbour has no objections to where you are proposing to build. It's always best to get those kinds of conversation out of the way before you start digging. Fencing can be hard enough to build in the first place, without having to move it all later on. Finally, you can check which of the boundary fences are your responsibility to maintain in the deeds of your house. If you don't get any joy that way, then the local planning office should be able to fill in any missing details.

Even if the fence in question is your responsibility, that doesn't mean it should look attractive only from your side. Far from it. The convention is that whenever you construct a boundary fence, or wall for that matter, you should always make sure the 'finished face' is on your neighbour's side. If you're building a fence that means the posts should be buried on your side of the panels; if you're building a wall that means the best pointing should be on the side you can't see. If it sounds a little unfair, just wait until the neighbours on the other side have to repair their fence, then you'll see the sense of it.

Prefabricated panels

If you're in any doubt as to what type of fence to build, I'd always suggest you opt for the tried and tested 'town and country' style lapped panel construction. These prefabricated timber panels come in a range of different colours and are simply nailed or screwed to wooden posts, or slotted down into grooved concrete posts, for assembly.

Wattle fencing looks wonderful in country-style gardens. Buy it in panels and attach to fence posts as on pages 40–3.

When you are building a fence of this type I would always recommend that you include 'gravel boards' in your design. These concrete panels or planks of tanalized wood sit along the bottom of each fencing panel and serve two important functions. Firstly, they act as kick boards to give the more delicate fencing panels above a measure of protection from the unwanted attentions of boots, balls, lawn mowers and the like. Secondly, whenever you are building a fence over soil you will come across the problems of damp and rot in the timber. Treated wood will now resist this for many years without complaining, but when the moisture does finally get to your fencing it will do so from the ground up. Replacing a rotting gravel board is a lot cheaper than buying a whole new fencing panel.

Trellises

The majority of fencing posts and panels come in heights suitable for most normal requirements around the garden. However, there may be occasions where you need to increase the height of your fence to provide

Conceal unsightly heaps of garden rubbish with screens of trellis and tubs of climbers.

some additional screening or privacy close to the house. A long run of overly high fencing panels may well block out nosy neighbours, but it will also block some of the light and breezes your garden needs to thrive. By far the best solution is to top off your panel fence arrangement with some ornamental trellis across the top. You can buy the trellis ready-sized for just such an application, in either straight or attractively arched configurations. Once secured in place, the trellis will provide some instant screening without appearing too 'offensive' to the other side. Later on, you can encourage some planting to grow up there which will further improve the effect.

Gates and doors

Now unless you are planning to live as a hermit or an eccentric recluse, the chances are you'll want to put some openings into your boundary walls and fences. Even where your walls or fences are purely decorative,

you may still want to create some gaps to dictate how people navigate around your garden. Whatever the purpose these openings can be large or small, and closed with anything from a small gate to a large set of double garage doors. Whatever the scale of the project in hand, there are some simple tips to make your life easier here. When you look at a timber gate or door it's often tempting to think 'I could make that'. Well, yes, you could, but you really don't want to. Not only are gates and doors actually far harder to make than they look, the slightest mistake you make when trying to build them exactly square will be exaggerated when you try to open them. Take it from me, there's now a whole range of ready-made gates and doors available, in everything from softwood to wrought iron, and all of them cost far less than you would end up paying in psychiatric fees if you aren't completely sure you know what you're doing.

The trick is, find your gate or door first and measure it up. Then build your fence with the appropriate-sized gap. Try it the other way around and you can have a very frustrating time. Also, when you're calculating the size of the gap you need to leave in the fence or wall, remember that you're going to need at least one gatepost fitted into that space, possibly two. Such posts are readily available in both metal and wood, or you can build one yourself out of brick. If you're using the popular concrete fencing posts for your project, you will find that most of these come pre-drilled with a number of holes through which you can simply bolt your gates into place. However, with front gates, or any opening that might take a hefty knock, it is never a good idea to hinge the gates directly on to the fence post or wall brickwork itself. One over-enthusiastic reversing manoeuvre and it's hello body shop, goodbye gates, and goodbye wall. At least with the gates mounted separately to the fence or wall you can limit the amount of damage you do to your home… Though, if it is at the front of the house, not to your pride, I'm afraid.

Refurbishment

Not all your projects will be new-build. You can often find fences or walls that have fallen into disrepair and need a bit of refurbishment to bring them up to scratch. Slight damage to walls, where the frost has eaten into the surface of a few bricks for example, can be remedied by chiselling the offending bricks out and mixing up some mortar to slot a matching-coloured replacement back in. More severe damage and you may have to demolish an entire part of the wall completely. In this case, check out some of the stone or bricklaying projects later on in this section of the book to get an idea of how you can rebuild to match the existing style.

Timber fences are usually a little easier to tackle. If the existing fence is a classic post and panel construction then you may be able to simply lift the damaged panels

out and drop some new ones back in place. If the original builder had the sense to fit gravel boards below each panel, then it might simply be a question of replacing the rotting or damaged planks with some new tanalized timbers. If the fence posts themselves are starting to rot at the base, then you have a bit more work to do. Dismantle the fence and pull all the posts up. If they're concreted into place, and you want to re-use them, just cut them off flush with the top of the concrete once they're out of the ground. If they're wooden, cut off the rotting section and treat the timber with preservative. A word of warning, they are now going to be much shorter than they were before. This will mean your old fence panels are too tall for your posts, so you could end up having to buy a new fence in any case. I would suggest that in many cases you are probably better off saving the panels, if they're still in good enough condition.

Here, a dull fence has been made into a focal point by cutting fencing planks in a variety of lengths.

Building brick walls

Most of the houses in Britain are still made out of brick and, in a lot of older properties, most of the garden walls are, too. If you want to construct a new wall (or refurbish an old one) that blends in with your existing environment then you're going to need to master a quick bit of bricklaying.

TIME

About 250 bricks per day

COST

approx. £100.00 per sq m (1sq yrd)

TOOLS

Wooden pegs and builder's line

Shovel and jointing iron

Spade, trowel, soft hand brush

Spirit level and square

15mm (½in) spacer

MATERIALS

Ballast and cement for concrete

Piece of 50 x 50mm (2 x 2in) timber

Vertical damp-proof course

Expansion board and pins

Bricks

Engineering bricks (optional)

Soft sand, cement and plasticizer

1

Whether you're building a free-standing wall or one that comes off an existing structure (as we are here) there's no escaping the golden rule. What goes up, must go down. Good, deep foundations are the key to a robust wall and that means digging a trench at least 60cm (2ft) deep to allow for 45cm (18in) of concrete and 15cm (6in) room for the first course of brick to remain below ground level. Use wooden pegs hammered into the ground and a builder's line or some string to mark out the eventual position of the wall, then use this as a guide to excavate the foundations. The general rule is to make your trench about twice as wide as the width of the wall it will support, and also about half the width of the wall longer at each end.

2

OK, you've dug your hole, now you've got to fill it up again… Mix up the concrete, 6 parts ballast to 1 part cement (see page 26), and don't throw in too much water – something about the consistency of gloss paint is what you're after. Work one wheelbarrow load at a time and start pouring from the end of the foundation trench where your new wall will need to match the height of existing brickwork. Get the depth of concrete adjusted here so that your first course of bricks will sit level with the existing below-ground brick course next to it. Use a spirit level and a bit of old 50 x 50mm (2 x 2in) timber to tamp down the rest of the concrete so that your final foundations are matched to this initial height. Finally, admire your work while it goes off, overnight in the summer or for about two days in the winter.

3

Now, if you're building a new wall that abutts an existing house wall you're going to need a vertical damp-proof course (DPC) and an expansion board – these are sandwiched between the old wall and the new one. They're both available in widths to suit the size of wall you're building, and need to be cut to length so that they also match the height of the new wall. First place the vertical DPC on the existing wall, and pin the expansion board into place to hold them both in position. Make sure you put them up accurately as you can then make pencil marks on the expansion board to give you a guide to where your new brick courses need to sit. (Line up a similarly marked batten at the other end of the new wall and you will make the bricklaying process much simpler still.)

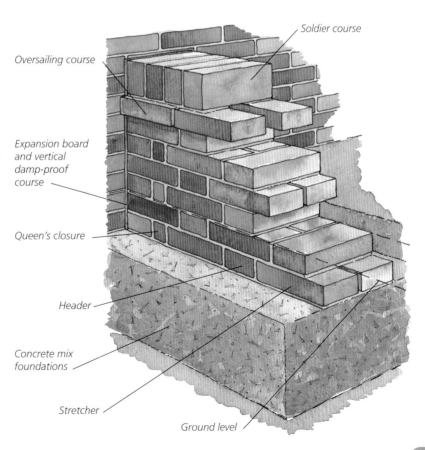

Soldier course

Oversailing course

Expansion board and vertical damp-proof course

Queen's closure

Header

Concrete mix foundations

Stretcher

Ground level

4

Use the pegs and builder's line to set out the 'face' of your wall. This will be the side that gets most attention so you don't want it weaving around. Also if you are coming off an existing structure at right angles, make sure the line really is at 90 degrees. Use a square to get it right. Position the line about 1 brick high and then loose-lay (i.e. with no mortar) the first course of bricks into place, using a 15mm (½in) spacer to allow for the mortar joints. It's a good idea to pick your bond style (the pattern in which you lay your bricks) at this stage. I've used a Flemish bond that includes quarter bricks inserted just in from the ends of every other course. These are called 'queen's closures' and are used to offset the bricks on alternate courses while keeping the length of each course the same.

5

It's finally time to start bricklaying. Mix up your mortar, 6 parts soft sand to 1 part cement (see page 26), and add a bit of plasticizer to keep it workable for longer. Again, work one wheelbarrow load at a time, and if it's hot cover the barrow with a sheet of wood to stop the mortar drying out too quickly. First trowel a 15mm (½in) layer of mortar on the foundation, starting from the end abutting the existing wall, and three bricks long (see **A**). Then, using your line as a guide and checking every so often with the spirit level as well, start bedding in the first course. You now need to introduce the 'stagger' of the bond. If this was a single-thickness wall, you'd do this by using half-bricks at either end; as this is double-thickness, you'll be laying the first brick sideways on.

Take the first brick and 'butter' its long side with about 15mm (½in) mortar (see tip box, opposite). Then lay it lengthways, its 'buttered' side pressed closely to the expansion board. Next add your first quarter bricks to form a queen's closure. 'Butter' one long side of each brick and lay them next to each other. Next, take two more full-size bricks, 'butter' one short side of each and lay them next to the quarter bricks (see **B**).

6

Going back to the end where you started, build up the next six courses. Trowel a 15mm (½in) layer of mortar on the top of the first bricks then start again, but this time start the course by 'buttering' the short ends of two ordinary-length bricks and pressing them up to the

expansion board. Don't worry too much about the excess mortar at this stage – just concentrate on getting the things straight and level. Then repeat the process at the other end of the wall. Once you have both ends built up this far, use pins pressed into the damp mortar and your taut line to stretch a guide along the length of the wall. Fill in all the central bricks along this guide, moving the line up each course as you progress. Keep the line nice and taut to make sure there's no sagging in the middle.

7

Once you're up about six courses and the central part of the wall is level with the two ends, go back down to the first course and start cleaning up the mortar, which should now be stiff enough to work.

Use a jointing iron (or the bend in a piece of 12mm copper pipe) to smooth a nice clean finish between each course, and then 'brush off the snots' with a soft hand brush (see **C**).

8

Using this method work your way up the entire wall until it has reached the height you desire. To finish off and weatherproof your new wall, you can add a course of engineering bricks, laid soldier-fashion along the top (see **E**). If you want to get really flash, you can even lay an oversailing course first as I have done here (see **D**). The overhang on each side, between the soldier course and the oversailing course, is a little cement fillet that stops any rainwater penetrating the top of the wall and keeps all the drips clear of the face. No rain, no stain. Professional or what?

BUTTERING A BRICK

'Buttering' is the term used in the trade for applying mortar to a brick. Holding the brick in one hand, trowel on a small amount of mortar, about the size of a dollop of ice cream, then, using the trowel, roughly shape the mortar so that the mortar is at its thickest in the middle, sloping off towards the edges.

D

E

Erecting panel fences

Fencing is one of the most immediate, dramatic and practical projects you can undertake in the garden. Panel fencing is one of the easiest ways to do it. Once you have grasped the principles and practicalities of the project I've shown you here, you'll find there are any number of different panel types you can use to make a fence exactly suited to your particular needs. As for posts: they're either wooden or concrete, and both have pros and cons. We've used concrete as it is much longer-lasting. Wood, while not so durable, is cheaper and – to many people – much easier on the eye. So, you pay your money…

TIME
1 day

COST
approx. £240.00 per 9m (30ft)

TOOLS
Builder's line or string
Saw, if using
Spade and shovel
Screwdriver and spirit level
Tape measure or cord

MATERIALS
Concrete fence posts
Screws
Ballast and cement for concrete
Gravel boards (optional)
Fence panels
Piece of 50 x 50mm (2 x 2in) timber for tamping down

1

Stretch out a builder's line or string to show the topmost run of your fence. If you're coming off an existing wall of the house, it's best to fix the line to the brickwork at exactly the finished height you want your panels to sit. Use a braced post (see tip box, page 43) at the other end of the intended fence line to stretch the line tight. The line must be both taut and unobstructed to make sure the fence will actually fit where you want it. Also, take care that the line doesn't stray into anyone else's garden – so you're actually allowed to build the fence where you want it.

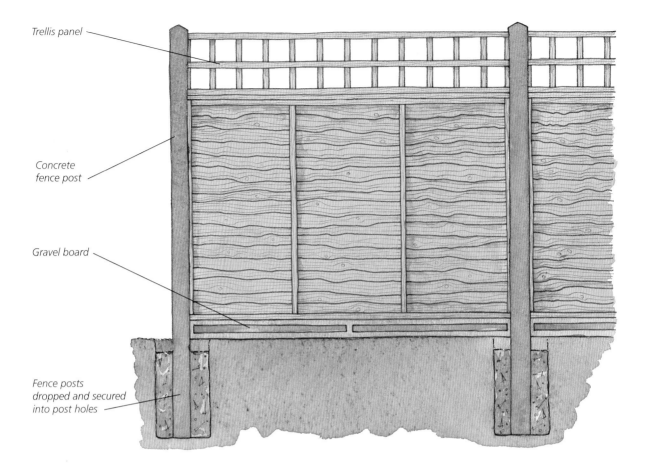

Trellis panel

Concrete
fence post

Gravel board

Fence posts
dropped and secured
into post holes

A

B

C

2

If you are working off the house, install your first post at that end. Each post must be bedded into a hole 30cm (12in) in diameter, dug to one-third the height of the finished fence. If you can't dig next to the house because of the foundations, screw-fix the first post on the wall. (The post will have to be wooden, even if your others are concrete.) You may have to saw a bit off the bottom to make sure it's the right height for the fence. If you can dig a hole for the post, drop it into place and brace it up exactly vertical in both planes. Fill the post hole to about 5cm (2in) below ground level with a 6 parts ballast to 1 part cement mix (see page 26), and move on to the next post location while that goes off.

3

Cut yourself a 'pinch stick' (a timber batten cut to size) the same length as your fencing panels and use this to mark off the centre of your next post hole from the first. (You can always use a tape measure or even a bit of cord if you don't have anything long enough to make the pinch stick – just make sure whatever you use doesn't stretch.) Dig this post hole out to the correct depth and then loosely brace your second fence post into place (see **A**).

4

If you've decided to use gravel boards (see page 33), place the first one into the groove in the second fence post and straighten it up across the ground with a spirit level. Pack it underneath to keep it level if you have to. Offer up your first fence panel (see **B**) and then brace both posts into place to hold everything tight. Fill the second post hole with concrete and move on to the next while that goes off. All post holes need to be filled with concrete to about 5cm (2in) below ground level so that you can hide everything under a little sprinkle of soil when you're done. Use a piece of 50 x 50mm (2 x 2in) timber to tamp down the concrete well into each hole (see **C**).

BRACING FENCE POSTS

Once you've bedded each fence post, and are happy it's straight, make sure it stays that way by nailing a couple of timber battens into the post, one on either side of your fence. The battens need to reach from the ground to the top of the panels (see page 120).

5

If your garden is straight and level, all you need do is carry on like this and the job's pretty much done. You may need to cut the last panel to fit the final gap, but apart from painting or treating the timber panels, that's it. You're a fencer. If your garden slopes, you'll have to calculate the drop you need between each post to accommodate the incline. The trick is to make sure each panel is level (see **D**) and the drops between the panels are exactly the same.

Bamboo screen

Bamboo screening is a delightful variation on traditional fencing techniques. The hardest thing in the whole project is finding a ready source for your rolls of bamboo. Larger garden centres should be able to help.

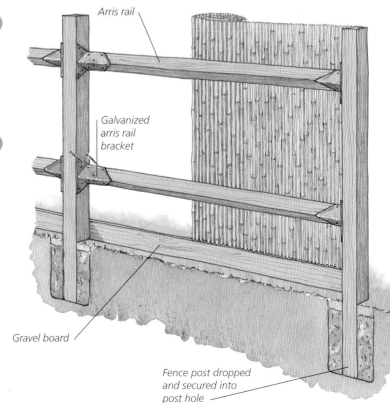

Arris rail

Galvanized arris rail bracket

Gravel board

Fence post dropped and secured into post hole

1

Just as I described for the panel fence project (see page 40), mark out the run of your new construction and bed in timber fence posts in the normal way, using a spirit level to ensure that everything is nice and straight. Your bamboo screen will eventually run flush with the top of these posts. As with the panel fencing, it's a good idea to use gravel boards at the base of the screen to give it added protection from damage and rot. Unlike concrete posts, wooden ones do not have a groove where you can just slot the gravel boards into place, so you'll first need to attach a strip of 25 x 25mm (1 x 1in) timber batten, the same height as the gravel boards, on to the insides of each post. The distance between your timber batten and the facing side of the fence needs to be the same as the width of your gravel board so that the board will eventually sit flush with the facing side of the fence. Fix your gravel boards to the batten using screws or nails. If you don't use gravel boards, you'll need to adjust the screen so that it sits about 5cm (2in) clear of the ground below.

2

You're now going to use lengths of timber called 'arris rails' to support the bamboo screen. These are square-section lengths that have been cut in half diagonally to produce triangular-shaped rails. Two of these rails are attached between each fence post – ideally, fixed in place using galvanized arris rail brackets that you can probably buy where you get the timber. These just nail or screw on to the posts – but cut and insert your rails before you do this. Alternatively, the rails can just be nailed or screwed directly to the posts themselves. Position the rails so that their largest flat face is flush with the facing side of the fence posts; fix one rail about 30cm (10in) down from the top of the post, and the other about 45cm (18in) up from the bottom (see **A**).

3

Using a staple gun, or just galvanized staples that you can hammer into place, fix one end of your bamboo roll to the first fence post and then start unrolling the rest. Fix the bamboo to both arris rails about every 30cm (12in) (see **B** and **C**). Any extra bamboo screen can simply be cut off the last roll when you get to the end of the fence. If the ground beneath your fence is going up and down all over the place, you can cut the bottom of the bamboo screen to match the contours, but always keep the top of the screen level.

Free-standing stone walls

Anyone who's travelled through Yorkshire and the Dales can't have failed to notice the amazing dry-stone walls that snake across the landscape in every direction. Building them without any kind of jointing mixture is a unique and ancient skill, but building something very similar with a barrow load of mortar at your disposal is a far easier proposition.

TIME

2 days

COST

approx. £50.00 per sq m (1 sq yrd)

TOOLS

Wooden pegs and builder's line

Spade, shovel and bolster chisel

Trowel, mallet and hammer

Spirit level

MATERIALS

Ballast and cement for concrete

Rocks and rubble

Soft sand and cement for mortar

1

As with any wall, the first stage is digging. Work out the position of your intended wall and use pegs and a builder's line or string to mark out the centre line. You need to dig a foundation trench that will take about 45cm (18in) of concrete and allow the first 15cm (6in) of wall to remain below the final level of the soil. The trench should be long enough and wide enough so that the concrete foundations extend about 15cm (6in) all around the finished wall.

2

Mix up your concrete, 6 parts ballast to 1 part cement (see page 26). Use just enough water to give it the consistency of gloss paint. Working one wheelbarrow load at a time, fill your foundation trench to about 45cm (18in) to create a flat and level surface on which to build the wall. Now don't get carried away with your walling and start work straight away – the concrete needs to be left at least overnight in the summer, or a couple of days in the winter, before it has gone off enough to build on.

3

In the meantime you can busy yourself with the selection of your main cornerstones (see **A**). You are going to create a wall made up of two parallel faces with rubble in between. Each of the faces will need a nice big stone at ground level each end. You need four large rocks which, ideally, are flat around a 90 degree corner. If you're buying rocks specifically for this project, then look out for examples that will form these corners. The other thing to bear in mind when you're selecting your rocks is that the base of the wall will be carrying more weight than the top, so earmark your biggest boulders for use in the first few courses. Finally, you'll need some nice flat stones to finish off the top surface of the wall, so put these to one side now.

4

OK, your foundations are firm and your rocks are all neatly sorted. Time to start walling. Mix up a barrow load of mortar, 6 parts soft sand to 1 part cement (see page 26), and keep it dry enough to support

the rocks as you work. Bed in your four big cornerstones to create both ends of the wall. You can use another line, pegged out to match one face of the wall, to act as a guide if you don't trust your eye at this stage. Now, while those rocks are setting firm, use smaller ones to lay out the entire first course in between. The only thing you need to worry about at this stage is how the finished rocks will look from the outside – all the space in the middle will just be filled with rubble and mortar.

5

Working one face at a time, use plenty of mortar to bed the rocks into place and trowel more mortar into the vertical spaces (see **B**). Once you have completed the first course of the second face, go back to where you started and scrape off the excess

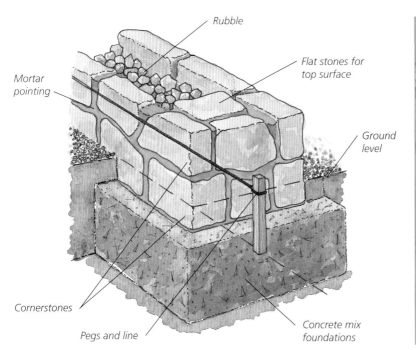

Rubble

Flat stones for top surface

Mortar pointing

Ground level

Cornerstones

Pegs and line

Concrete mix foundations

C

mortar between the rocks. Ideally, you want to end up with a little convex V-shape along all the joins – to do this, run the point of your trowel along the top and the bottom of the mortar (see **C**). If the mortar is too runny to shape in this way, then carry on with the building work until it has gone off a little more.

6

Using this technique (lay out dry, bed in one course at a time, and point each face of each course once the mortar's stiff enough before you move on to the next), you can continue right up to the top of your wall (see **D**). As you go, chuck all the little bits of rock and rubble into the gap between the two faces and slop in a good measure of mortar as well.

As you reach the top of the wall, leave the level of this infill about 15cm (6in) below the rocks on either side. With a final load of mortar and the flat stones which you carefully selected for the top of the wall (you did put them to one side, didn't you?), finish off the construction to create a nice level surface all along the top (see **E**).

7

Finally, wait until the last of your mortar has gone slightly stiff and finish off the pointing to complete your new wall (see **F**). If your subsequent celebrations involve dancing or drinking anywhere near the construction site, I suggest you postpone them for at least a couple of days to let everything firm up.

ADDING FENCE PANELS

If you'd like to add a bit of extra height or decoration to your wall, why not add some fence panels as we have on page 46? When you come to the top 30cm (12in) of your construction, bed in some short fence posts to the mortar infill. The spacing of these posts will depend on what you fix between them, but most garden centres or DIY sheds have a fine selection of trellis or hurdle-type panels – we used wattle fencing for our stone wall. Pick the one you like best, then cut and position your supporting posts to accommodate their length.

Turfing

Unless you're planning to turn the garden into a lake or a car park, the chances are you'll end up with a fair amount of lawn. Whether you're patching up existing grass, or laying a whole new area the right way to turf is something well worth knowing. Here I'm going to show you how to roll out an average-sized lawn, laid next to the house. You can simply scale this technique up or down to suit the particular area you have in mind.

TIME

1 day

COST

approx. £3.50 per sq m (1 sq yrd)

TOOLS

Fork or hired Rotovator

Spade and rake

Wooden pegs and builder's line

Sledgehammer

Half-moon edging iron

String or sand

MATERIALS

Rolls of turf

Scaffold boards

Fine topsoil and sharp sand, if using

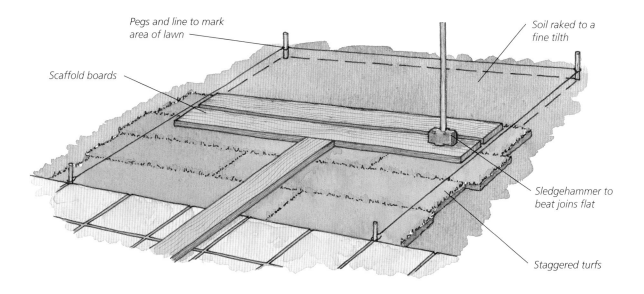

Pegs and line to mark area of lawn

Scaffold boards

Soil raked to a fine tilth

Sledgehammer to beat joins flat

Staggered turfs

1

The first job with any turfing project is to prepare the soil. If you're just turfing a small area this can be done with a garden fork, but if you have something bigger in mind you're best off hiring in a Rotovator. Whatever you use, all the soil needs to be lifted, broken up and then levelled. While you're at it, weed out the plantlife then get a decent rake and drag out all the large stones. Rake them into piles and then, if you haven't got any other little project in mind for them, bury the stones in holes under the soil – this also helps the drainage. You want to leave yourself what's called a 'fine tilth', loose soil free from weeds and stones. This needs to be fairly level; you can use an old scaffold plank laid across the soil to check this, but there's no substitute for some good old forkwork to get it flat in the first place.

2

Use pegs and a builder's line or string to mark out the edges of the finished lawn then, starting from the end nearest the house, start to roll out the turfs. Lay them so that they roll out widthways across the garden – this disguises the lines when looking from the house – and stagger the positions in each row (like laying bricks) so that the ends of the rolls never sit alongside each other. The edges of the rolls should be pressed up closely to each other. Using your pegged lines as a guide, lay the turf so that it goes about 5cm (2in) beyond the finished edge of the lawn all around (see **A**).

3

As you progress down the garden, the main thing to avoid is treading on the newly laid turfs. Lay two scaffold boards across the width of the lawn to stand on as you work, and then keep rolling them over each other to follow the turf as you go. Lay further scaffold boards down lengthways to reach these first boards as you get further from the house – that way you'll never have to tread on the grass itself (see **B**). As you complete each row of turfs, lay one of your two widthways scaffold boards over the line where the rows meet and use a sledgehammer to beat the joints flat (see **C**).

4

Once the whole area has been turfed, including the 5cm (2in) overlap all around, the next thing you have to do is wait. If you're laying your lawn in summer you can give it a mow after two weeks and once a week after that during the growing season, but the lawn will take at least two months to really settle in. If it's warm weather, use a sprinkler to keep the turfs damp, especially during the first couple of weeks they're down, and don't be tempted to walk on it more than necessary at this stage.

5

Well watered and well bedded in, once two to three months have passed you can think about edge-shaping the lawn. Use a half-moon edging iron to cut the lawn to its final dimensions, using the pegged lines (they are still there, aren't they?) as a guide. If you want to create a more ornate edging at this stage you can sprinkle down some sand or lay out some string to give you a curved cut line to follow. If you see any gaps that have opened up between the turfs, use a mix of 1 part fine topsoil and 1 part sharp sand to pour into these holes. The grass will soon grow and leave you with a perfect new lawn.

PAVING THE WAY

If you think of your garden as a little city, and imagine all the grass, planting and water features as great places to play in and to visit, then your hard-landscaping provides the essential function of getting you around and giving you somewhere to park yourself to enjoy the view. Paths and patios are vital to a successful garden, and deciding on their location and construction is every bit as important as your grand planting plan. Obviously the location and orientation of your hard-landscaped areas is essential to the overall look and feel of the garden, but the unseen construction techniques that lie below are crucial to the longevity of all your great plans.

Gravel (above right) is a great material for use on garden paths, especially if the ground isn't level. Paving slabs (right) are more difficult to lay, but will stand up well to heavy use.

In simple terms, the materials and construction techniques you choose to employ for a path or paving project are a direct result of the kind of traffic you think that area will receive. A little path around the back of a potting shed that only gets visited once a month is a very different undertaking from a front drive on which to park your fully restored traction engine. Fortunately there's now a huge range of materials on the market from which you can select the most suitable finish for the job in hand – from bark chips or gravel for a simple sprinkled path, to concrete or wooden stepping stones for a more decorative affair, from crazy paving or brick paviors for a small patio right up to full-blown tarmac or cobblestones for a heavy-duty driveway.

As with all hard-landscaping projects in the garden, if in doubt assume the worst and cater for that eventuality. It may take a little more time and a little more material to build your patio on 10cm (4in) foundations rather than 5cm (2in), but it will save a lot of heartache later on when you find your weekly line-dancing parties are starting to

cause subsidence all over the place. The other thing to remember is that well-laid hard-landscaping will last for many years, so put down the best materials you can afford. There are plenty of places where you can economize, but your choice of paving surface shouldn't be one of them. Large paths and patios can take a lot of work and a fair amount of money to get right, but they can also make a stunning difference to the aesthetics and the practicalities of your garden environment. The golden rule is to take your time and get everything right when paths and patios are going down, so that you won't ever have to suffer the frustration of taking them up again to make repairs.

Paving surfaces

Now for all the myriad materials that will tempt you while you wander the DIY shed, paths and patios are made of just two distinct types of surface: stuff that drains, and stuff that don't. Stuff that drains includes gravel or shingle, bark chips, wooden tiles and even temporary plastic paving that you can simply roll out across the lawn as a route for the wheelbarrow. The reason these all drain is because they are placed directly on to compacted sand or soil without any impervious materials underneath that would stop water simply soaking away. Because of this, there is no need to make any great effort to ensure the land is flat or even sloping. The material itself will compensate for any lumps or bumps and all the water will disappear into the ground long before it has a chance to well up in puddles. Usually employed for 'low traffic' path projects, these types of finish are pretty cheap to buy, quick to create and will successfully keep a path dry underfoot when the grass around is still slippery and muddy. Also, in a rustic or woodland-type garden, there's nothing more sympathetic than some nice log stepping stones with a bark chip surround winding their way between the bushes. These types of material also lend themselves very readily to being mixed in unusual eye-catching combinations.

Patios are easy to construct and don't require much maintenance.

However, no surface made purely with these materials is designed to withstand a lot of regular use or heavy pedestrian traffic, and the loose materials they employ can soon be kicked all over the flower beds and the lawn by determined young feet. Once you are beyond the limitations of these rudimentary surfaces you must enter the world of non-porous materials: a world of hardcore and 'whacker plates', silver sand and spirit levels. A world that always seems flat, but is never quite level…

By far the majority of paths and patios are actually made from materials that won't allow water to drain through them. These include such surfaces as poured concrete, stone paving slabs, brick paviors and decorative cobblestones. These types of material are employed where the area is going to take some heavy usage, and are all laid on some form of foundation layer below. The depth and the density of those foundations are determined by the weight that the finished structure will have to bear.

Drainage

To provide adequate and effective drainage when building in this way, all path and patio projects have to include a 'fall'. This is a slight slope across the entire finished surface, which will ensure that excess water not only runs off but runs off in the right direction. Calculating the direction and the angle of this fall is not too difficult (see page 58).

Building a path in this way is usually pretty straightforward. Even if the path is flat over the entire length of its run, it's easy enough to ensure that it slopes very slightly to one side along the way, so spilling the surface water on to the grass or flower beds nearby. Building a large patio in this way is less easy. Obviously, if you're building a hard-landscaped area that adjoins the house you don't want the surface tilted towards it. Not only that, you need to make sure that even the highest part of your new patio is at least 15cm (6in) below the existing damp-proof course in your house wall. Tilting the patio away from the house and towards a lawn or flower bed is the obvious solution but, if this is not practical in your garden, then make sure you are sending the surface water towards an area where you have made adequate provision for drainage. Remember, a large paved area can collect a lot of water when it's raining hard, and all that water's got to go somewhere.

Creating a slope

The angle of the fall needn't be that great: about 1 in 100 is fine – or 1cm every metre (⅜in every yard). The important thing is to keep that angle consistent. It's useless to have your 1 in 100 drop perfect across most of the patio, only to have the edge rise up where it meets the lawn. That is the recipe for an unscheduled water feature. There's no way of ensuring that the fall of your patio will be right, other than getting the angle of your foundations right and then constantly checking with a taut string and spirit level as you lay the top surface material in place.

Where you are working over a particularly large area and can't rake the foundation bedding material to the desired angle with a long scaffolding plank or the like, you should hammer a network of pegs into the ground (all about 2 metres/6ft apart) and, using a taut string and spirit level, ensure that all their tops are flush with the desired foundation height. From there on in you know that as soon as your mortar or concrete is up to the top of the pegs your foundations are following the intended angle of fall.

Foundations

When creating foundations for paving or patios, don't ever get wooed into that 'out of sight, out of mind' mentality. Think more along the lines that if you shirk on what's out

Paving slabs don't have to butt up to each other. These spaced slabs surrounded by gravel are an attractive alternative.

of sight then you are almost certainly out of your mind. You may be digging in the baking heat of midsummer, on soil that you can hardly get a pickaxe into let alone a spade, but if the project you're working on calls for 10cm (4in) foundations of hardcore you make sure you dig them. If you end up going down further, all the better. Come wintertime the soil in your garden, and in particular the soil under your new patio, will become swollen with moisture. Anything built on top of it will be under pressure to move upwards and outwards. If all you've got up there are a few skimpy little paving slabs, then that's exactly what some of them will do. Then, in the summer, when the soil dries out again and shrinks down in height and volume, your already wonky paving slabs will be squeezed back together with such force that some of them could even crack or ride up. All that is without even considering the pressures your patio will be under from all the kids and overweight relations stamping about on top. A decent, well-made foundation protects your patio from both directions at once. It provides a solid 'slab' of immovable material that will fend off the seasonally shifting soil below and evenly distribute the weight of party poundings from above.

Ideally, when laying foundations that require compacting down into place, it's best to construct some wooden shuttering around the entire perimeter. This is just some long planks, nailed on to pegs hammered into the ground, which create a temporary but solid wall around the foundation material to stop it spreading out as you flatten it down. This shuttering can be left in place while you lay the actual paving material, as it will provide a nice straight edge to butt the slabs or paviors up against. When you've finished this part of the project, whether you've employed shuttering or not, you might like to complete it with some decorative edging.

Edgings

Much undervalued today, a brick or tiled edging to hard-landscaped areas can have a visual and practical impact on your work. Now available in many different guises, from log roll to roll-topped tiles, soldier-course bricks to artificial stone strips, natural or man-made edging blocks should be considered as the frame around your patio painting. Not only will it provide the eye with a defined boundary, a properly designed edge can be used to stop loose paving material such as gravel being spilled on to the lawn, or indeed stop soil from a flower bed spreading over a neighbouring path. If you're creating hard-landscaping next to a lawn, try to ensure that the highest part of what you're building is never higher than the grass itself. When you cut the lawn your mower will then pass right over the man-made areas, enabling you to trim right up to the edge of the grass without any tedious recourse to strimmers and the like.

Here, shaped slabs surrounded by pavior edging create a seating area visually separate from the main patio.

Paving stone patio

If you've got a garden you'll almost certainly want a patio. This simple formula has kept most of the garden builders I know in business for years. Laying a paving stone (slab) patio is quicker and simpler than you think. As with most things, it's all in the preparation.

TIME
1½–2 days

COST
approx. £7.00 per sq m (1 sq yrd)

TOOLS
Wooden pegs and builder's line

Spade, hammer and bolster chisel

Spirit level
(plus straight length of timber)

Jointing iron and soft hand brush

Trowel, shovel and rubber mallet

6mm (¼in) spacer

MATERIALS
Paving slabs

Sharp sand, soft sand and cement
for mortar

Soft sand and cement for pointing

Plasticizer

1

The biggest problem anyone has with a patio is drainage. If it's surrounded by grass poor drainage can just mean puddles, but if it's up against the house it can be disastrous. The solution is simple. Most houses will have a damp-proof course (DPC) running around the bottom of the walls, which won't let any water rise through it from the bricks below and thereby protects all the bricks above. To keep your DPC working properly, make sure the surface of your new patio is at least 15cm (6in) below it, and then make sure the patio slopes away from the house to keep all the run-off rainwater in the garden and not slopping about next to the wall. With all this in mind, use pegs and a builder's line, or string, to mark the edges of your patio and then excavate the soil to provide a firm foundation. If your patio is just meant for people and parties you need to dig down only about twice the depth of the paving slabs. However, if you want to run cars over the surface, you're going to need to go down at least four times the depth of the paving slabs, pour in some concrete and then bed your slabs on mortar. We don't need that kind of foundation here, but I'd dig out with a spade rather than a fork to keep the compacted soil in place (see **A**).

2

As you dig, use a spirit level and a straight length of timber to ensure the fall of the land slopes gently away from the house. Then before you start laying the paving slabs, mark out this fall with an accurately pegged line (see page 58).

3

Loose-lay the first row of slabs closest to the house, using a 6mm (¼in) spacer to keep the gaps even as you go. Mix up a barrow load of mortar with 4 parts sharp sand, 2 parts soft sand and 1 part cement (see page 26). Not too much water – you want it supple enough to tap the slabs down into it, but firm enough to hold them still when in position. Add a little plasticizer to keep the mortar workable for longer. Bed in the two slabs at either end of the row, get them to the right height, then string a line between them as a guide for the other slabs in that row (see **B**). Use a trowel to spread your mortar out, score some grooves into it, then tap each slab into place with a rubber mallet (see **C**). Work row by row, away from the house, guided by the peg line (see **D**).

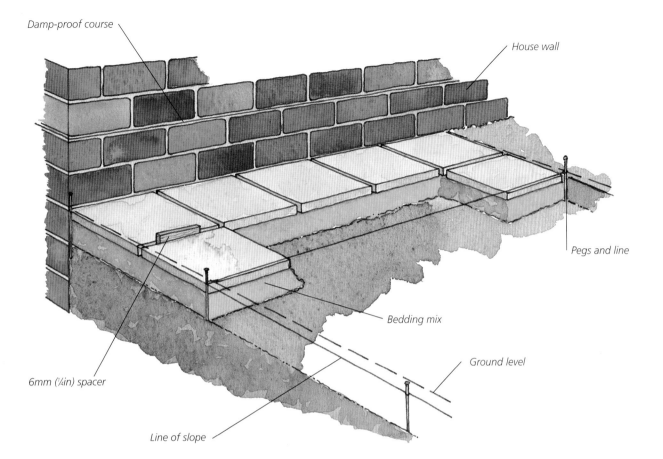

Damp-proof course

House wall

Pegs and line

Bedding mix

Ground level

6mm (¼in) spacer

Line of slope

D

4

When all your slabs are down, leave the whole thing for a day to go off. To fill in all the spaces between the slabs, mix up 3 parts soft sand with 1 part cement (no water) and brush this into the gaps. The trick is to first take the rose off your watering can and pour water directly into all the gaps. Wait until any water left on the surface of the slabs has dried off and then brush in your pointing mixture.

TYPES OF PAVING SLAB

If you don't want to use natural stone paving slabs you can buy man-made alternatives which look almost as good. I would suggest, though, that natural stone weathers more attractively in the long term. As to the size of slabs you should buy, larger slabs will cover the ground more quickly and economically, but small slabs give you greater flexibility with the pattern in which you lay them.

Ornamental paving

There was a time when patios had an image that was 'square'. This was largely because the only paving slabs you could buy were, well… square. Those days are long gone. You can now go to any decent-sized garden centre and pick up a whole range of slabs in a variety of shapes and sizes, which can then be combined to create a patio that is far more attractive than the 'drab slabs' of yesteryear.

TIME

2 days

COST

approx. £200.00

TOOLS

Wooden pegs and builder's line

Sand to outline area

Spade, shovel and trowel

Rubber mallet

7.5 x 2.5cm (3 x 1in) piece of timber, 2m (6ft) long and spirit level

Jointing iron

MATERIALS

Ornamental paving slabs

Sharp sand, soft sand and cement for mortar

Plasticizer

Soft sand and cement for pointing

1

Ornamental paving usually looks best surrounded by lawn or flower beds. However, if you want your patio next to the house, make sure the surface of the patio is at least 15cm (6in) below the damp-proof course and that it slopes away from the house (see page 58).

2

Having decided on the layout and the position of your patio – it might be worth loose-laying the whole thing out at this stage to make sure you're happy with the design (see **A**) – use pegs and a builder's line or string to mark it all out. If your chosen design is circular, you can always hammer a peg into the centre point and then stretch out a line from that to the correct radius. Using this as a guide, walk around the central peg, keeping the line taut, and sprinkle sand to create a rough circle for your excavations. Once you have the whole area marked out, use a shovel to scrape off about 15cm (6in) of topsoil, leaving the compacted earth below undisturbed. If you are planning on a 'feature edging', which needs to be buried further down than the rest of the patio, make allowance for that now and dig your foundations deeper around the outside of the excavations.

3

String out a couple of lines that cross at what will be the centre of your patio, and adjust these with a spirit level so that you can use them as a guide to keep everything flat. Now, starting from the middle slab, loose-lay your design a few slabs at a time and begin to bed them into place (see **B**).

4

Mix up a barrow load of mortar with 4 parts sharp sand, 2 parts soft sand and 1 part cement (see page 26). Keep the mix quite wet – you want it supple enough to tap the slabs down into it, but firm enough to hold them still once in position. Add a little plasticizer to keep the mortar workable. Spread out your mortar with a trowel, score some grooves into it and then tap each slab into place with a mallet. Use a straight piece of timber about 7.5 x 2.5cm (3 x 1in) and 2m (6ft) long to check all the slabs are flat and in line.

5

If you're creating a feature edging, you'll need to bed that in last, using the finished design of slabs as a guide. When everything's in position, leave the whole patio for at least a day to go off. Then, to fill in all the spaces between the slabs, mix up 3 parts soft sand with 1 part cement (no water) and brush this into the gaps. The trick here is to first take the rose off your watering can and pour water directly into all the gaps. Wait until any water left on the surface of the slabs has dried off and then brush in your pointing mixture. Tidy up the joins by going over them with the tip of a trowel, a proper jointing iron, or even the bend in a piece of 12mm copper pipe (see **C**).

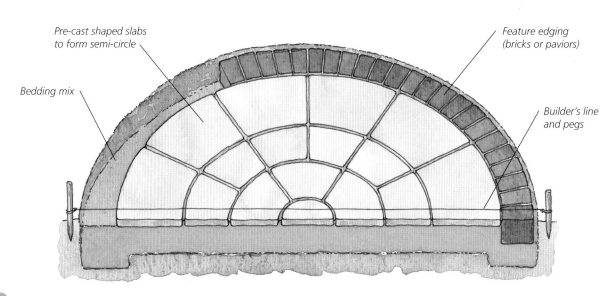

Pre-cast shaped slabs to form semi-circle

Feature edging (bricks or paviors)

Bedding mix

Builder's line and pegs

Brick pavior patio

Brick paviors are smaller than traditional paving slabs, so they take longer to lay. Because of their size you can arrange them in a greater variety of patterns, or 'bonds', so the end result is potentially more attractive. They're an expensive way to fill large areas, but for small patios or decorative paths they're easy to lay and very hardwearing.

TIME
2 days

COST
approx. £45.00 per sq m (1 sq yrd)

TOOLS
Wooden pegs and builder's line
Spade, shovel, hammer and bolster chisel
Hired whacker plate
Rubber mallet, trowel and spirit level

MATERIALS
Sharp sand, soft sand, cement and plasticizer for mortar
Brick paviors
Sharp sand for patio area
Kiln-dried sand for pointing

1

As with all paved areas, you must always be conscious of the drainage implications of what you're building. In my many years of experience I've noticed one key thing to help you here: water always runs downhill... So make sure all your surfaces are either sloping towards the garden or towards the nearest drain (see page 58). Most important of all, if you are building next to the house, don't let any of your surfaces come any higher than 15cm (6in) below the existing damp-proof course (DPC).

2

Mark out the position and fall of your patio with pegs and a builder's line or string. Your foundations need to go down at least 10cm (4in), twice that if you intend to run vehicles over the finished surface. Once the soil has been removed (use a spade rather than a fork to keep the compacted earth below undisturbed), you can string a line to mark out the position of your edging paviors.

3

Mix up some mortar with 4 parts sharp sand, 2 parts soft sand and 1 part cement (see page 26). Not too much water – it must be firm enough to hold the edging paviors still once they are in position. Add a little plasticizer to keep the mortar pliable, and work with one wheelbarrow load at a time. Using your line as a guide, bed in all the edging paviors on to the soil below (see **A**). Use plenty of mortar underneath, but butt the paviors together with no mortar in the gaps. These edging paviors

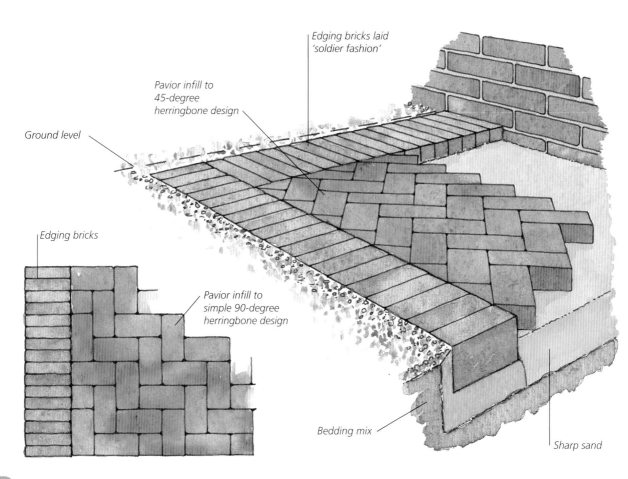

Edging bricks laid 'soldier fashion'

Pavior infill to 45-degree herringbone design

Ground level

Edging bricks

Pavior infill to simple 90-degree herringbone design

Bedding mix

Sharp sand

should be laid 'soldier fashion', and can be adjusted so that the finished height of the edging is either flush with the patio or even just below it. Add another line of mortar along the bottom of the outside edge to keep everything firm. Once all the edging is in place leave it for at least one summer's night or two winter days to go off.

4

Once all the mortar is firm, fill the whole patio area with enough sharp sand to leave the level about half-way up the edging paviors. Now hire a vibrating whacker plate and run it across the sharp sand until you end up with a firm, flat surface which will hold a pavior about 1cm (½in) above the height of the finished patio. A whacker plate is just a sheet of metal with an engine and a handle. The engine vibrates the plate, while the weight of the machine presses down on the ground beneath it. You can get manual compactors, but you need to like hard work to use them on a large patio surface.

5

Working away from your pile of paviors, so that you don't have to keep traipsing across the sand, start filling in the whole area with the pattern or 'bond' of your choice (see **B**). Lay in all the whole paviors

first and then cut the others (with a hammer and bolster chisel) to fill the gaps. You should end up with a tightly packed surface, butted hard up against the edging all the way around.

6

Now sprinkle the whole area with kiln-dried sand (i.e. fine as well as dry) and sweep as much of it into the gaps as you can. Get the whacker plate out again and vibrate all the loose sand into the gaps, adding more sand as you need it. Finally (once the all the paviors are down at their finished level and all the gaps are completely full of sand) brush off the leftover sand, get out the garden furniture, open a beer and enjoy…

CUTTING BRICK PAVIORS

Whatever type of patterns you lay with brick paviors the chances are you're going to have to cut a few to finish off. If they're just straight cuts then this can be done with a hammer and bolster chisel, but you might need to practice on a few first to get your technique right. For angled cutting, easier and far neater is to hire a guillotine-type cutter made specially for the job. You can also use an angle grinder, but use the right cutting disk and always wear strong gloves and safety goggles.

Cottage path with steps

It would be a nice easy world if all the paths I had to build were straight – but it would also be a rather boring one. Whether the lie of the land demands it or not, adding a few curves to your paths makes them far more interesting to look at. This project shows you a quick way to add some wiggle to your walkways without resorting to specially shaped slabs.

TIME
1 day

COST
approx. £25.00 per 3m (10ft) run

TOOLS
Wooden pegs and builder's line
Spade and shovel
Spirit level
Wooden spacer
Trowel and jointing iron

MATERIALS
Sand or chalk for marking area
Paving slabs
Pebbles and shingle
Sharp sand, soft sand and cement for mortar
Soft sand and cement for pointing

1

Clear all the weeds or vegetation from the run of your path and then roughly mark out the two lines it will follow by sprinkling down some sand or chalk. You can use a 'pinch stick' cut to the width of the finished path to ensure these two lines remain pretty much parallel all the way along. Stand back to have a look at everything from a distance every so often, to check it's all heading where you want it.

2

Use a spade to skim off the top 5cm (2in) of topsoil, leaving the compacted earth beneath undisturbed. You can also take this opportunity to level out any slight lumps or dips along the way. Once you're done, loose-lay the entire path with slabs to get some idea of the gaps and angles you'll need to create between them.

3

Working one barrow load at a time, mix up some mortar with 4 parts sharp sand, 2 parts soft sand and 1 part cement (see page 26). Working from one end of the path to the other, begin to bed in your slabs on about 2.5–5cm (1–2in) of mortar (see **A**). Make sure it doesn't squeeze up through the gaps and, if you have a fairly long straight run, use a little wooden spacer to ensure that all the gaps between the slabs are consistent.

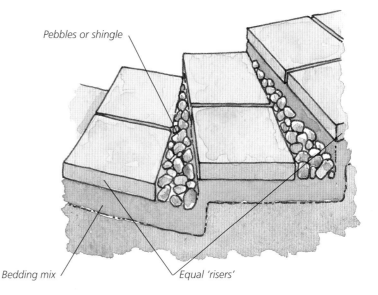

Pebbles or shingle

Bedding mix

Equal 'risers'

4

Where you need to curve the path, lay in a generous amount of mortar and then press in some little pebbles to decorate the bends (see **B**). Press them in far enough to hold firm, but not so far that they all but disappear below the mortar!

5

You'll need to create steps if a slope is too steep for a normal path. On a fairly gentle incline you can just slop in some extra mortar (nice firm mix) to support the slabs. Where the fall is too great for this, you'll need to dig into the earth with a spade and make some rough soil steps, then trowel on sufficient mortar to support the slabs in position (see **C**). If the fall is even greater, dig out the soil to form a series of little terraces all the way down and then build a small retaining wall at the front of each terrace. Once the retaining wall is dry and firm, backfill the step with plenty of mortar and lay your slabs on to that. The important thing is to keep the height or 'riser' of each step constant.

6

Once the mortar has been left to go off for either one summer's night or a couple of winter days, you're ready to start pointing. Mix up 3 parts soft sand with 1 part cement (no water) and brush this into the gaps. The trick here is to first take the rose off your watering can, then pour water directly into all the gaps. Wait until any water left on the surface of the slabs has dried off and then brush in your pointing mixture. Tidy up the joins by going over them with a jointing iron or the bend in a piece of 12mm copper pipe.

Yorkshire stone steps

Quick to build, strong and great to look at, these steps are an eye-catching feature for any garden. The actual construction is pretty straightforward; the trick to making them as picturesque as they are practical is all down to the selection of your stones and the pattern you build them into. Also, with a technique like this that doesn't involve creating proper foundations, I wouldn't recommend you try a flight any longer than about three steps.

TIME

2 days

COST

approx. £40.00 per step

TOOLS

Spade

Saw, hammer and bolster chisel

Wooden pegs

Spirit level

Trowel and rubber mallet

MATERIALS

Wooden planks for shuttering

Yorkshire stone or other local stone

Sharp sand, soft sand and cement for mortar

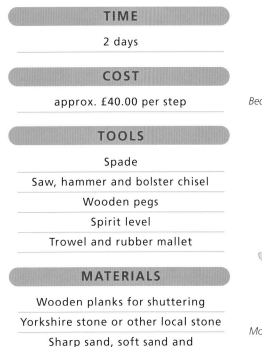

Wooden shuttering

Bedding mix

Mortar pointing

Flat stones for top surface

1

Use a spade to excavate the slope into a number of evenly spaced terraces. Try to avoid disturbing any more of the soil than you have to so that all the compacted earth underneath remains untouched.

2

Next, prepare some shuttering. Cut a wooden plank the height and width of each intended step and then hammer pegs into the ground to secure these shutters flush against what will be the front face of each step. Make sure the height of each step is exactly the same as all the others. Use a spirit level when you tap the shutters down into place to keep all the steps flat and horizontally level.

3

Pick out your best cornerstones and lay them on the soil at each end of every shutter. You're looking for rocks that have a nice 90-degree angle around one corner and an attractive pattern on what will be the front face. Sort out some nice flat stones at this stage for the upper surface of each of your finished steps.

4

OK – rock picking done, rock sticking about to begin… Mix up some mortar, 4 parts sharp sand, 2 parts soft sand and 1 part cement

(see page 26). Add enough water to make a firm consistency that will hold the stones in place. Begin by bedding in the front cornerstones on each step. Press them well down into some mortar and hard up against the back of each shuttering board. Pack more mortar behind them as you go. From there, work your way across the whole front face, which on a small step may take only one more large flat stone. As you go, try to create an attractive arrangement with the rocks and organize them so the flat faces are always pressed up against the shuttering. Don't use so much mortar at this stage that it squeezes out on to the front surface. You'll be pointing the gaps later.

5

Once the main rocks on the front of each step have been completed, fill in any spaces left above so that the mortar level is brought up flush with

the top of the shuttering. Use some more small rocks if any of these spaces are too big for a blob of mortar to fill. Now, take those nice flat stones that you carefully put to one side earlier and bed them down into place on the horizontal face of the step (see **A** and **B**). Tap the rocks down and check with a spirit level to leave a lovely smooth surface on top.

6

Leave the mortar to go off for one summer's night or two winter days, and then remove the shuttering. Finally, mix up another load of 4:2:1 mortar and use a trowel to point all the gaps. You want to try and end up with a neat convex V-shape of mortar between each rock – run the point of your trowel along the top and bottom of the mortar. Wait two to three more days for this to go off, then run up and down the new steps to your heart's content.

TIMBER DECKS

Warm to the touch, cheap to maintain, easy to lay, and you can walk all over it…
Intrigued? It is, of course, decking. Now you may have noticed that we use a lot of decking projects in *Ground Force*. I like decking. Decking is fantastic. Not only is it great to look at, but you can also take the most unlikely and depressing corners of your garden and transform them into a practical area that will serve you well for many years to come. And you can forget about all that laborious levelling and slab-sloping that a well drained patio requires of you. Decks are quick and flexible, and the rain runs right through them. Best of all, decks are the most amazing fun to build. Once you've worked out how to construct the foundation layer of joists, the rest is all plain sailing. You'll quickly come to realize that the design and function of your potential deck are limited only by your ambitions and your imagination.

Now there was a time when everyone thought decks meant expensive hardwood planking. I'm pleased to say that's just not true any more. Both you and your local rainforest will be delighted to know that there is now quite a range of treated softwoods available for this kind of outdoor construction, and the various galvanized fixtures you need to put the whole thing together are to be found in most of the big DIY stores. Another great aspect of this construction system is that the tactics and techniques for building decks don't really alter with the scale of the design, so once you've mastered the steps and instructions that follow you'll be ready to tackle pretty much anything the size of your garden and the size of your budget will allow. In fact, now I come to think about it, the only downside I can see with this whole decking

High-level decks (left) are a good way to provide a level seating area over sloping land. Low-level decks (below) look lovely when surrounded by contrasting textures such as pebbles or plants.

game is that it's so quick and easy to knock up one of quite a decent size, that just when you're really getting into the swing of things and are itching to start another one, you'll find the garden's already full!

OK, first things first. Decking means timber. Big decks mean lots of timber, so at the risk of repeating myself, you need to make sure you are buying the right timber in the first place. From what was once a construction technique popular only in the USA, Scandinavia and New Zealand, decking is quickly making its mark in the UK. Inevitably, this means more and more manufacturers are offering an ever greater variety of timber and fixings with which to complete your projects. Mostly this is great stuff – occasionally it isn't. Decks are pretty simple things to build and what you need to build them with is pretty straightforward too. Here is the plain and simple Tommy guide to what you need to buy…You can build a deck entirely out of one size of timber if pushed, but it is far more likely that you will end up using three.

Posts

High-level decks are held above ground level by timber posts. These are usually 100 x 100mm (4 x 4in), but if you are planning something where areas of the deck are going to be more than 2 metres (6ft) above ground level you'll want to increase this dimension to posts that are 150 x 150mm (6 x 6in).

Joists

Both high-level and low-level decks are supported on a base construction of joists. Usually this framework is constructed from 150 x 50mm (6 x 2in) timber. However, this dimension depends on how close together the joists are placed and how often they are supported on posts or 'padstone' foundations. I recommend that you build a framework with joists no more than 40cm (16in) apart. Each of these joists needs to be supported from below at less than 3 metre (10ft) intervals and with these dimensions you'll be fine with 150 x 50mm (6 x 2in) joists. However, if

for some reason you had to make the supports from below more like 3 metres (10ft) apart, then your joists would need to be 200 x 50mm (8 x 2in) to provide the same strength. If you want to get into the maths in any great detail there are plenty of books you can get from the shops which will bore you more rigid than the deck itself.

Another great thing you can do with decking joists is to extend them beyond your last vertical support. Say, for instance, you were building a raised deck on the side of a slope. At one end it would be supported at ground level, but at the other end it could be cantilevered high above the sloping ground below, with the outer edge of the deck well beyond the outermost vertical support. In cases like this you should never take the joists out past

This elaborate high-level deck incorporates a raised platform with a decking 'path' leading up to it.

the last point of support by any more than one-quarter of their entire length.

Decking boards

Finally, once you've completed your framework of joists, you will lay the decking boards. These usually come in one of two sizes: 150 x 25mm (6 x 1in), which are quicker to lay and cover the joists with less fixing, or 100 x 25mm (4 x 1in), which take longer to lay (because you need more of them) but arguably look nicer once they're down. Again, these sizes are affected by the actual construction details of your deck, but unless you are laying the boards on to joists that are more than 40cm (16in) apart you won't need to step up to 50mm (2in) thick timber.

Fittings

Most decks are held together with a mixture of bolts, screws and nails, but there are an increasing number of fittings that provide easy-fix methods of attaching anything from a right-angle joist to an angled stair-tread. The combination you need will depend on the type of structure you are building. All you really need to remember is this. Always use galvanized fixings because these will resist rust once they're in and are therefore much less likely to stain your wood. When you're fixing down the decking boards use either galvanized ring nails or galvanized screws – nothing else will do. Also, whether you're using nails or screws, drill a pilot hole for each fixing to ensure that it goes in straight and true.

Decorative options

When you're thinking about the decking boards, remember there are a number of options open to you. Many DIY sheds and timber yards now stock decking boards that are smooth, grooved or even coloured. Smooth boards always look slightly more natural, but the grooved alternatives offer better grip when the wood is wet. Coloured can be interesting, but it might be as well to build the deck first and then decide if you want to colour the boards when you've had a chance to see it in place for a while.

The direction of your decking is also a decorative option. Just because you've built the deck square on to the house it doesn't mean the boards have to run that way as well. Fixing the decking boards down on the diagonal can be very effective indeed. In fact, you can even combine areas of the deck where the boards go in different directions on the same surface. Two things to remember, though. Firstly, the most economical and efficient way to deck out a framework of joists is at right angles to that frame. Start putting your boards down at odd angles and you will increase the amount of timber required to complete the same area. You need to take this into consideration when quantifying your project. Secondly, no matter which way you lay the boards, make sure you've decided before the joists go down, not after. Decking boards need to be laid at right angles to the joists that cross the supporting frame. If you are planning to have decking boards going in more than one direction on the same framework your joists will have to be constructed to allow for this.

Whatever option you choose, you will need to secure your deck in place so that there are no wayward wobbles. For this, there is no substitute for rock-solid and regular fixings into the ground below. Any soleplate (supporting joist) or upright post must be resting on firm footings, and even when you think the framework of

Give your deck a Mediterranean feel with brightly coloured paints. You should use exterior paints for a lasting effect.

joists is ready for decking give it one last check by bouncing on the joists wherever you are furthest from a vertical support. If there's still movement, chock the joists up underneath with more padstones or timber. The best tactic of all to keep the deck rigid is to mount it off something solid, like the wall of your house. Be warned, though: if you are planning to attach a wall-plate to your house then make sure you either place it at least 15cm (6in) below the damp-proof course or mount it in such a way that the wall behind it is fully protected from any damp that may migrate across.

Variations

If you're feeling particularly adventurous with your decking designs, you might want to try incorporating some existing garden features into the plan. Let's say you want to build a nice big deck off the back of the house, but you quickly come slap-bang into a large tree right in the way. Rather than reaching for the chain saw, reach for the jigsaw instead. It takes a little more effort to cut your joists and decking boards so that they flow around a large object like a tree, but the final result is well worth the time and effort. In fact I like the result so much I occasionally build an opening into a deck so that a tree can be planted there later on.

Low-level decks can sometimes be no more than simple platforms a few centimetres above the grass, but high-level decks can be very much more elaborate. If your structure is going up much more than 60cm (2ft) you should consider the safety and aesthetic advantages of steps and balustrading. While it is possible to add both steps and balustrading to a deck after it has been constructed, this is far from ideal. It is much better to work these features into the original design and then construct your deck to support and accommodate them. Balustrading, for example, can be supported from elongated support posts that come right up from the foundations, while stairways are best built on to specially positioned joists which protrude from beneath the deck. The stairways

themselves can usually be constructed from more of the same timber used elsewhere in the deck. However, the balustrading always poses more of a problem. If you're lucky, you may well find some off-the-shelf products, intended for internal staircases, which match the timber of your deck. However, if you can't find an exact match for the decking timber you might look at staining the balustrading to match, or even painting it a different colour. Alternatively, you can always order up some smaller sizes of timber when you get the main decking boards and build the balustrade from scratch.

You might even think about using some trellis from the garden centre to create an attractive barrier around your new deck. Get some plants growing over that and you could be forgiven for thinking you'd emigrated to the Deep South of America. Add a rocking chair, a shotgun and some country and western music and you have it all…

You don't have to lay your decking boards at right angles to the joists. Diagonally laid boards make this expanse of deck look much more interesting.

Low-level decks

Over the past few years decking has become more and more popular in this country and all the materials you need to build a deck are now readily available at most good timber yards. The beauty of decking is that it's quite quick to construct and doesn't need slopes and drains. Provided any part of the deck that abutts the house is below the damp-proof course, rainwater will drop through the slats and soak away.

TIME

2 days

COST

approx. £280.00

TOOLS

Spade and saw

Spirit level

Straightedge

Drill and Screwdriver

Hammer

Handsaw/powersaw

MATERIALS

Ballast and cement for concrete

Bricks or blocks

Nails

Tanalized timber for supporting joists, 100 x 50mm (4 x 2in)

Timber for joists, 150 x 50mm (6 x 2in)

Tanalized timber planks, 150 x 25mm (6 x 1in) or 100 x 25mm (4 x 1in)

Screws

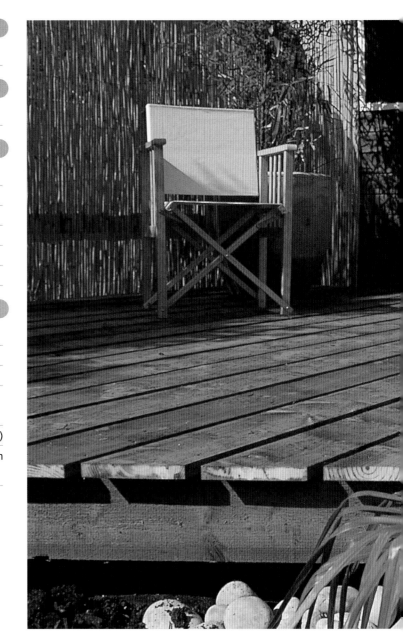

1

Work out the size and orientation of your finished deck, clear your chosen site of all that garden debris and plant material you've previously dumped there and get your spade out for a quick bit of digging and levelling.

At this stage all you want to ensure is that there are no major lumps or slopes in the soil. Once your deck is down, you don't really want any part of the timber to be in direct contact with the earth below – that's where the rot sets in.

2

You're soon going to lay a network of structural 100 x 50mm (4 x 2in) soleplates, around the entire perimeter and, possibly, across the middle of your site. These will need to be supported above the soil level about every 1.5m (5ft) and to do this you'll need to build some padstone foundations. Measure and mark out the final positions of the joists (see page 78), then dig out a 30cm (12in) cube of soil wherever you need a padstone support. Half-fill these holes with concrete (6 parts ballast to 1 part cement) – see page 26 – and wait for it all to harden.

3

Using bricks or blocks, a little more mortar and a long spirit level, build up solid piers on each concrete platform until you have a nice little crop of firm foundations, all of which are exactly level with each other. Wait for the concrete to fully harden (two days in winter, overnight in summer), then cut and place your soleplates so that they span all the padstones. These timbers can be simply nailed together where they meet and just rest down on to the padstones (see **A**). You don't want your construction to span gaps larger than about 2m (6ft) between soleplates. If you're creating a fairly large deck with additional soleplates across the middle of your site, they must run in the same direction as the decking boards.

4

You now have a firm and level timber base on which to build the rest of your deck. Next up are the 150 x 50mm (6 x 2in) joists. Laid at 90 degrees to the soleplates and therefore 90 degrees to your final decking boards, these timbers need to be nailed to the soleplates below every 35–40cm (15in) across the site (see **B**). Lay the joists overlength (see **C**) and then use a long straightedge to mark an even cutting line about 2.5cm (1in) proud of the perimeter soleplate. Use a handsaw to cut off the excess at the end of each joist.

5

Once your joists are in place it's time to walk the plank… Bounce about to see if there's any distortion in the frame. You should nail a central line of 150 x 50mm (6 x 2in) pieces of timber (called 'noggins') between the joists to correct any sideways movement (see **D**) and if your deck is large you may need two rows or more. Pack more bricks under anywhere that drops. That done, it's time to lay the decking boards.

6

Using either 150 x 25mm (6 x 1in) or 100 x 25mm (4 x 1in) tanalized timber planks, cut your boards slightly overlength and start fixing them on to the joists (see **E**). If you are building your deck next to the house then I would start there and

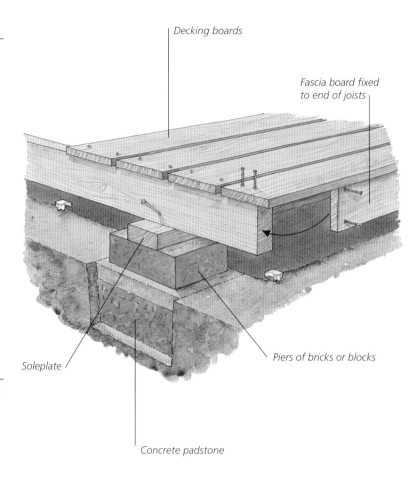

Decking boards

Fascia board fixed to end of joists

Piers of bricks or blocks

Soleplate

Concrete padstone

work away from the wall. Pre-drill the boards where you are going to nail through them; if you're using screws make sure the heads are countersunk into the timber. Use small offcuts from the decking boards to create some 2.5cm (1in) spacers to separate the planks as you fix them in place. This gap can be varied, but don't make it too small for decent drainage, and don't make it so large you lose the cat. Unless you are very confident about your measurements at this stage, it's a good idea to loose-lay all the boards in place. That way you can adjust the gaps between them so that everything is evenly spaced and exactly fills the deck area without the need to cut any board along its length.

7

Once everything's in place, use the straightedge or chalk line again to mark a cutting line along the ends of the boards about 5cm (2in) out from the joists underneath. Use a powersaw or handsaw to cut off the excess at either end of the deck. (I actually prefer a handsaw for this job as it gives you a much cleaner and straighter cut.)

8

Finally, use some more of your decking boards to create fascia panels to hide the exposed joists. If you cut the 5cm (2in) overlap on the edge of your deck correctly this fascia panel will end up exactly 2.5cm (1in) in from the edge of the deck. If you didn't, this is where you'll find out.

High-level decks

Designed to even out the contours of your garden and reclaim previously impractical areas for level living, high-level decks are particularly effective where you have a garden that slopes away from the house.

TIME
2–3 days

COST
approx. £550.00

TOOLS
Spade
Straightedge or chalk line
Spirit level
Drill and hammer
Screwdriver
Handsaw/powersaw

MATERIALS
Ballast and cement for concrete
Tanalized timber posts, 100 x 100mm (4 x 4in)
Timber for joists, 150 x 50mm (6 x 2in)
Tanalized timber planks, 150 x 25mm (6 x 1in) or 100 x 25mm (4 x 1in)
Nails and screws

1

Work out the dimensions and orientation of your deck, then clear the site of all plants and debris.

2

Measure out the framework of joists you will need to construct to support the deck, then decide where to place your padstones (see page 78). Each one will support an upright post, on to which the frame of joists will be secured. You'll need one padstone at each corner of the site, one under any point where three or more joists will meet, and then at intermediate sites to ensure no part of the structure is unsupported for anything more than a 2m (6ft) span. Dig out a 30cm (12in) cube of soil where each padstone will sit, then fill the hole with concrete (6 parts ballast to 1 part cement) – see page 26. If you are building a deck that abutts the house then screw or bolt a 150 x 50mm (6 x 2in) wallplate on to the brickwork (see **A**) and support the joists at that end.

3

After the concrete has gone off (two days in winter, overnight in summer), you're ready to place tanalized timber posts on to these foundations. You could use 100 x 100mm (4 x 4in) fence posts for this or even round lengths of timber but, whatever you opt for, leave everything longer than you need at this stage. The posts just rest on to the padstones, and won't become rigid until you incorporate them into the construction of the framework that they support.

4

Using 150 x 50mm (6 x 2in) tanalized timber joists, nailed together where they meet and mortised into the upright posts where they occur, create a perfectly level framework that spans the entire area of your deck (see **B** and **C**). This network of joists should never leave gaps of more than about 40cm (16in) for the subsequent deck to span, and make sure all your internal joists ran at 90 degrees to the direction of your final decking boards.

5

Once all your joists are in place it's time to walk the plank… Bounce about a bit to see if there's any sagging or distortion in the frame.

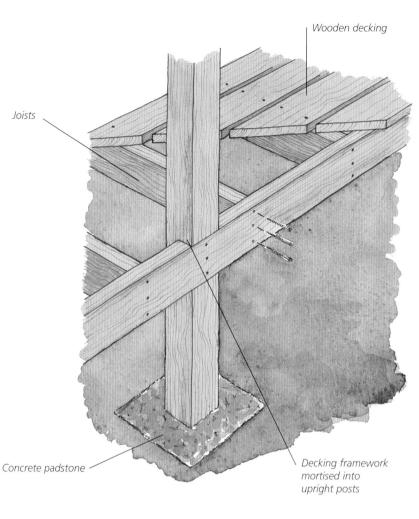

Wooden decking

Joists

Concrete padstone

Decking framework mortised into upright posts

You should stiffen the frame by nailing in a central line of 150 x 50mm (6 x 2in) pieces of timber ('noggins') between the joists. If your deck is very large you may need two rows or more. Add 100 x 100mm (4 x 4in) timber uprights under anywhere that still sags or drops. When you do this, lift the frame of joists a little – you can lever it up with a length of 150 x 50mm (6 x 2in) timber – so that the timber you are using to pack out the frame goes in just slightly too high. The weight of the joist frame will press it back down level when you lower it. Now it's time to lay the decking boards.

6

Using either 150 x 25mm (6 x 1in) or 100 x 25mm (4 x 1in) tanalized timber planks, cut your boards slightly overlength and start fixing them on to the joists. If your deck is next to the house I would start there and work away from the wall. Pre-drill the boards where you are going to nail through them; if you're using screws make sure the heads are countersunk into the timber. (It's your toes if you don't.) Use small offcuts from the decking boards to create some 2.5cm (1in) spacers to separate the planks as you fix them in place. The gap can be varied, but has to be large enough for decent drainage, though not so large that it's a hazard for the unwary.

7

Once everything's in place, use the straightedge or chalk line to mark a cutting line along the ends of the boards about 2.5cm (1in) out from the joists underneath. Use a powersaw if you must, but preferably a handsaw, to cut off the excess at either end of the deck.

FURNITURE
and FEATURES

There was a time when gardens were just for growing things, and then weeding them out again. The only other life you'd find there were dogs and kids. How much things have changed since then! Books and television shows over recent years have catalogued and encouraged the transformation of our outdoor spaces from temporary summer quarters to practically year-round extensions of the house itself. This changing attitude has also resulted in a steady avalanche of products and information, all intended to get us out into that fresh air more often and more easily.

FAR LEFT: Window boxes are an ideal way of adding colour to a dull windowsill.

LEFT: Garden structure kits are quick to construct and a cheaper option than the ready-assembled alternatives.

RIGHT: A dull-looking garden seat can be transformed with a coat of paint.

So far, this book has mainly been concerned with how we create large weather-resistant areas in the garden and how we move around in them once they're built. But there is much more to outdoor DIY than that. If we are all now using the garden as our 'outside room' then it stands to reason that we'll want to furnish it and decorate it just like any other part of the house. Furniture and decorative features are what we're talking about, and can encompass a huge range of fun and practical projects for you to try out. For the family to live and eat outside you need everything from storage areas to a full-blown dining table. For the plants to enjoy themselves as well, you'll need raised beds and climbing frames. For the garden as a whole to come alive, there's nothing better than a quick decorative arch, or a rather more ambitious pergola. When you've patioed, paved and planted everything there is to be seen, but your tool shed is still

calling to you, this is the chapter to get stuck into. Projects such as those that follow make a great way to pass an afternoon, or even an entire weekend. And, like most of the other ideas featured in this book, each will provide you with the skills and techniques to create bigger and better projects of your own.

Every garden centre now has a huge selection of chairs, tables, umbrellas and the like for use outside, most of which are very good quality and very good value. However, whatever you buy ready-made for your particular garden will always be to some degree a compromise. You might find a chair that's just the right size, but not quite the colour you had in mind. Maybe there's a table made in all the right materials to complement your patio space, but it's just that bit too long… or too narrow… or too low. The only sure way to get furniture that is exactly what you want for exactly where you want it is to build it yourself. Not only is this far more practical than you might imagine, it is also a very satisfying project to undertake. Take something like a table: how many people can labour away for a weekend and create something that will provide a hub around which friends can gather for years to come?

My only word of warning is that if the space in your garden is limited, and you can't leave your furniture in place all year round, you might want to opt for some kind of shop-bought folding furniture instead. You can make chairs and tables that collapse (ideally not while you're eating), but your carpentry skills have to be fairly well

Rather than concealing a shed, why not make it a feature? Paint it in a bright colour to complement the rest of your garden.

developed to attempt that. Again, the construction techniques for the garden table shown later in this book are solid and straightforward. If you enjoy that project and want to get your saw teeth into something similar, try your hand at making some chairs in a similar style. A little time and planning with paper and pencil should produce a design that is every bit as pleasing as the table itself.

Prefabricated structures

Also readily available from the DIY sheds are prefabricated garden structures such as arches and pergolas. (I describe a prefab arbour later on.) You'll quickly realize that these kinds of structure are fairly easy to make and work out far more cost-effective. The only thing to remember with these features is that while you may think of them as primarily decorative, they should actually have a practical part to play in the garden. Nothing looks more incongruous than a bewildered little pergola, stuck right in the middle of the lawn. In general, these types of construction are best suited to the edges, the paths or the secret corner of your garden and they always look far better when there's a bit of greenery growing over the timbers.

Stability

And don't forget that even a small garden feature will carry a fair bit of weight when it's planted up, and will provide a large surface area for any strong winds that may come calling. The bigger the structure you build, the more it has to be anchored into the soil below. The general rule is 25 per cent of any vertical post should be below ground. So what looks like a 2 metre (6ft) post should in fact be nearer 2.5 metres (8ft), with about 60cm (2ft) out of sight in the soil. With small arches and the like, burying the posts is usually enough, but when you come to large free-standing pergolas you should start thinking about concrete, or a ready-to-use powder that sets rock hard when water is added, down in those holes to keep everything nice and stable. Also, you will find that adding exterior wood glue to all your joints will have a dramatic effect on the rigidity of larger structures. Finally, if you're planting climbers around your feature, give them all the help you can. Adding trellis to the sides and top of your timber structures will not only improve the privacy and shelter inside, it will also provide a welcome foothold for all those outstretched tendrils.

Plant supports

You can of course create structures that are just intended to support the growing plants and nothing else. In these cases, the design priorities are a bit different. Something

With a little knowledge of carpentry, gazebos are relatively simple to construct. They are then a wonderful place to relax.

like an arch or pergola will remain a visible feature in the garden all year round, while a support for climbing plants is successful if it completely disappears. Plant supports can be either free-standing, such as the obelisk project later on, or mounted on to a wall that you want to hide behind greenery. Free-standing plant supports can be as simple as a wooden post sunk into the ground. If you're feeling particularly generous you could always stretch some garden wire between nails at the top and bottom of the post. A little more elaborate, and a little more work, are timber 'wigwam' type structures. These can be anything from a few splayed sticks tied at the top, to a full-blown tower of trellis. The trick is to match the structure to the plant that has to grow on them.

Vigorous vegetables such as peas and beans can find their way up pretty much anything, while slower-growing flowers need the help of regular horizontal battens to thrive.

If you're intending to attach a trellis straight to the wall, don't. Plants need space on both sides of a trellis to grow and climb, so you should always screw wooden battens to the wall first and then nail your trellis on to those. Ideally you want the finished trellis to be about 2.5–5cm (1–2in) away from the surface of the bricks. Once down the garden centre, you will soon notice that trellis comes in many different varieties: square-shaped, diamond-shaped, rigid, expanding, straight, curved and fanned. In general the shape of the trellis is a purely aesthetic decision – provided the plants can reach the next bit easily enough they couldn't care less about the pattern. What you do need to consider, though, is the materials from which the trellis is made. Timber is best used where the structure is likely to remain on view – a large pergola, for example. Green plastic or coated wire trellis is for use where you want the plants to take over completely and lose all sight of what's holding them up – usually the wall of a house.

Beds and containers

It's all very well providing adventure playgrounds for your plants to enjoy, but if there's nothing for them to grow out of then you're rather wasting your time. As hard-landscaping in the garden becomes more and more popular, so too do enclosed beds and free-standing containers for the plants that you want to grow there. Both planting systems provide a very attractive solution to the problem of bringing greenery into the built parts of your environment. Enclosed beds are usually brick or timber surrounds that lift the level of the soil in one particular area, but still allow the plants to root into the earth below. On a large patio, or around the borders of a

If you're creating a garden, why not choose a theme for it? This teahouse would make a wonderful basis for an oriental garden.

This shed has been transformed into a delightful seating area by the addition of an attractive raised deck.

garden, raised beds can look stunning. Not only are they great on the eye, allowing flowers to cascade down over the edges, but they are at a much more practical height to weed and maintain. Larger beds can even be expanded to create seating around the built-up edges and, used intelligently, an arrangement of raised beds can help create those all-important 'rooms' within the otherwise open space of your garden.

Even more flexible are free-standing planting containers. Basically, they're structures that lift the plants clear of the soil below – they might be anything from an old bucket to a handmade wooden trough. Whether used inside or out, up on a windowsill or down by the pond, up on the balcony or underneath the porch, planting containers can bring colour and life to any part of your home – even if you don't have a garden. There are plenty of shops where you can buy suitable tubs and the like, or better still you can make your own. You can

even make containers from the heap of junk at the bottom of your garden – that butler's sink you chucked out, for example, or even that old bath! Just make sure you keep the look of the container in keeping with the feel of its surroundings.

It is also important that all your containers have drainage holes underneath, so that the plants don't have to sit in water all day when you've been too enthusiastic with the hose. All containers are best filled with a layer of stones or broken pots at the bottom to keep the drainage holes clear, followed by your soil or compost. Even in a small container this can soon add up to quite a weight, so position your container while it's empty, and then fill it up once it's there. The size of your containers is limited only by your construction talents, but if you have any intention of taking the finished items with you if you move, think of the removals men before you start building.

Instant arbour

There was a time when any decorative garden structure had to be built in standard lengths of tanalized timber. Thankfully, those days are gone. You can now get the most attractively designed constructions in kit form, which just need unpacking and nailing together. However, to make sure they don't then revert to their kit form when you least expect it, here are a few tips to keep your arbours upright.

TIME
3 hours

COST
approx. £180.00

TOOLS
Screwdriver/hammer
Spirit level and square
Spade and shovel
Paintbrush

MATERIALS
Kit-form arbour
Screws/nails
Ballast and cement for concrete, if using
Exterior wood stain or timber preservative

1

Having finally realized that you'll never fit the kit-form arbour in the car (without leaving the kids at the garden centre) and had the thing delivered instead, the first step is to unpack all the bits close to where you want the finished construction to stand, and then check everything you need is there.

2

Now, start assembling the wall panels and the roof, but don't drive any of the fixings in too far – just a few turns if it's held together with screws, a couple of taps if it's nails. Also, where there are two or three fixings for one panel, use just one of them for now (see **A**).

3

Once the walls and roof are in place, lay the arbour on its front, line everything up using a 90-degree square at the corners, and then fix the back panel into place. Once you're sure all the angles are right, drive home all the fixings that secure the back panel in place (see **B**). (If anyone moans that your arbour looks a bit wonky, the key word here is 'rustic'. It means 'I wanted it to look like that, now stop complaining'.)

4

You will now need help to lift the arbour upright and use a spirit level to make any final tweaks to the angles. Keeping the shape right, attach the diagonal braces and drive home all the remaining fixings to firm everything up (see **C**).

5

Next, you need to carry the finished structure to its exact position in the garden and mark where each of the legs will stand. Move the arbour to one side and dig out post holes to match these marks. Drop the arbour back into place and use either concrete (6 parts ballast to 1 part cement) – see page 26 – or just soil to pack the legs so that your arbour is both level and secure.

6

Finally, use an exterior wood stain or timber preservative to make sure all your hard work lasts for years to come.

Diagonal braces

Legs dropped and secured into post holes

Lean-to pergola

If you have a patio next to the house then this is a great project to make that area of your garden into something quite spectacular. Not only does a pergola give your plants something new to explore and make their own, it will also provide a lovely shaded spot where you can eat and relax in dappled summer sunshine.

TOOLS

Spade and shovel

Drill

Handsaw

Spirit level and square

Nail or bradawl

Screwdriver

Chisels

Chalk line

Paintbrush

MATERIALS

Tanalized timber,
150 x 50mm (6 x 2in)

Timber batten,
50 x 25mm (2 x 1in)

Tanalized timber,
100 x 100mm (4 x 4in),
for the uprights

Screws, including
four 75mm (3in) wood screws
and nails

Rawl-bolts or anchor bolts

Soil or half-bricks for
steadying uprights

Ballast and cement
for concrete

Paint or timber preservative

1

The first thing to do is decide on the angle your roofline will follow. The deciding factors here are that you need to leave at least 2 metres (6ft 6in) headroom at the lowest point (usually the side furthest from the house) and that you need to have a clear span of brickwork on which to fix your wall-plate (usually decided by your first-floor windowsills). You should aim to have a roofline for the pergola that falls from about 2.5 to 2.1 metres (8 to 7ft) as it stretches away from the house. However, depending on the length of your roof beams, you'll have to see what looks best for the scale of construction you have in mind.

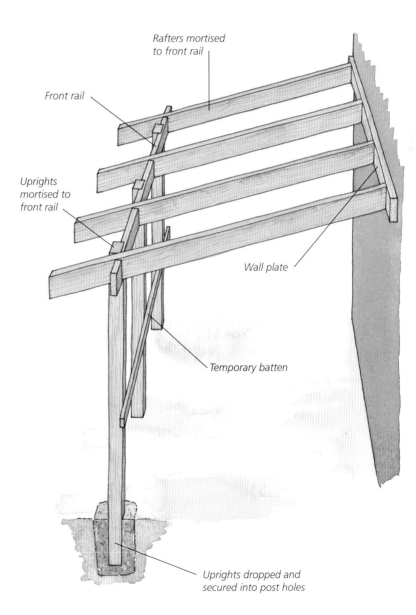

Rafters mortised
to front rail

Front rail

Uprights
mortised to
front rail

Wall plate

Temporary batten

Uprights dropped and
secured into post holes

2

Now cut a wall-plate from 150 x 50mm (6 x 2in) tanalized timber to the width of your finished pergola (see **A**). Starting about 15cm (6in) in from one end, and making marks every 1.5m (5ft), drill a series of holes through the centre line of the wall-plate. The size of these holes will depend upon the type of masonry fixing you are using to hold the wall-plate in position, but you should really be looking for either rawl-bolts or anchor bolts to do this job properly.

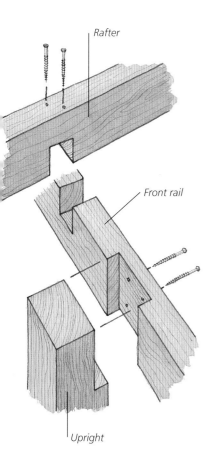

Rafter

Front rail

Upright

3

Get some willing volunteers to hold the wall-plate up in its final position and use a spirit level to make sure it's straight. Now, making sure the wall-plate doesn't move, use a nail or a bradawl to mark through the holes in the wall-plate into the wall behind. Remove the wall-plate and use a masonry bit on your drill to make holes wherever you made a mark. Finally, lift your wall-plate back into position and secure it into the drilled holes with your fixings. If you have either a particularly large wall-plate, or a depressingly small circle of friends, you may need to adopt another tactic when fixing your wall-plate. A small timber batten (say 50 x 25mm/2 x 1in) can be screwed on to the wall using the technique above and placed so as to support the far larger wall-plate while you mark and fix it into place. You don't

even need to take the timber batten off when you're done – it all adds to the strength of construction. Indeed a second little batten, screwed along the bottom of the face of the wall-plate, will help to stop the rafters dropping at this end.

4

Having fixed the wall-plate into place, you can now turn your attention to the front frame. Using 100 x 100mm (4 x 4in) tanalized timber posts for the uprights and 150 x 50mm (6 x 2in) tanalized planks for the top rail, it's best to build this frame flat on the ground somewhere you have room to work (see **B**). Cut all the timber to length (allowing an extra 30cm/12in for each upright to sit in a post hole) and mark a 150 x 25mm (6 x 1in 'mortise' to cut out at the top of each upright post. Where these posts meet the front rail (about every 2m/6ft along is fine) mark, cut and then chisel out a 150 x 50mm (6 x 2in) 'tenon' in the front rail for the post mortise to slot into. Use a square to make sure your uprights are indeed upright, and then screw the front frame together with four 75mm/3in wood screws at each mortise and tenon joint.

5

You're now going to lift the front frame into place, but before you do you'll need to screw or nail a temporary 50 x 25mm (2 x 1in) timber batten across all the uprights (about 1m/3ft up from the bottom), and another batten across each top corner (see **C**). Carry the front frame to its final position and mark where each upright will stand. Dig 30cm (1ft) post holes for the uprights, then drop the front frame back into the

holes; use soil or half-bricks in each post hole to make sure the frame is level (see **D**) and then firmly brace it into an exactly upright position using planks nailed to each side or even resting across the top.

6

Cut your first rafter out of 150 x 50mm (6 x 2in) tanalized timber, but leave it about 15cm (6in) longer than you'll eventually want, including the 30cm (1ft) or so that will overhang the front frame. Take this rafter down to one end of your pergola and offer it up against the end of the wall-plate and the end of the front rail. Mark a vertical line down the end of the rafter that matches up with the front face of the wall-plate and the end that matches the back face of the front rail. Take down the rafter and cut down the line that matches up with

the wall-plate. Then, using the line that matches the front rail as a guide, mark another parallel line 5cm (2in) beyond that to give you the profile where the rafter will line up with the front rail. Measure up 5cm (2in) from the underside of this profile and cut and chisel out a notch from the rafter. You should now have a rafter which is cut at the house end to match the angle at which it joins the wall-plate, and notched at the other end where it will sit over the front rail. Use this rafter as a template to cut all your other rafters to match. I'd suggest you cut enough to place them about every 1m (3ft) across the entire width of the pergola.

7

Now, mark on your front rail where each of the rafters will sit then cut and chisel out a 5cm (2in) notch

that will marry up to the notch in each rafter (see **E**). To position these rafters, mark the first two about 15cm (6in) in from each end of the pergola and then spread the rest evenly along the remaining space.

8

Drop all the rafters into place, fixing as you go (see **F**). One screw down through the notched join at the front end is fine, with another screw driven in at an angle where the rafter meets the wall-plate near the house. It's always best to drill a little pilot hole for these screws to make sure they end up where you want them to go in.

9

Now fix the uprights into position by filling the post holes with either concrete (6 parts ballast to 1 part cement) – see page 26 – or the ready-to-use powder you pour in dry

and then add water to set it hard – a kind of instant cement. Finally, mark or snap a chalk line across the front ends of the rafters about 30cm (1ft) out from the front frame.

Drop a plumb line down to mark a vertical cut line and then saw all the rafters to length. Add some paint or timber preservative and you're done.

Raised timber bed

Now, much as I'm a fan of hard-landscaping in the garden, there's always a danger that you might go just that bit too far and end up with one huge patio. Here's a great project that will enable you to inject some greenery back into the landscape, giving you plants above the soil even when you can't get to it below.

TIME
1 day

COST
approx. £90.00 for a 3 x 2m
(10 x 5 ft) bed

TOOLS
Square

Drill and screwdriver

Saw

Paintbrush

MATERIALS
Tanalized timber, 150 x 50mm
(6 x 2in)

Screws

Pins, if using

Exterior paint or
timber preservative

1

If you're building one of these beds on to an area of existing hard-landscaping, pick a spot that's nice and flat, with enough room for you to walk around the finished raised area. If you're building a bed directly on to soil, make sure it's clear and level before you start.

2

Use four lengths of 150 x 50mm (6 x 2in) tanalized timber to create the first ground-level frame for your raised bed. Make this frame to the exact size and shape that you require for the bed. Use a square to make sure it's all straight, and then secure it with a couple of screws in the ends of each long side (see **A**). As ever, it's best to drill pilot holes for all screw fixings in this project to make sure the screws go in straight and true.

3

Now build up the subsequent frames for your bed in the same way until you have a loosely stacked construction to the height you require. For both the look and the strength of the thing, I suggest that you make each alternate frame in an opposite fashion to the previous and subsequent levels – 'log-cabin' style (see **B**). So, for example, if your first frame is secured with screws into the ends of each long side, then your next frame should be secured with screws into the ends of each short side, and so on all the way up. (This is still true if you are making a square bed, where all the sides are the same length, but life is too short for me to try and explain it that way…)

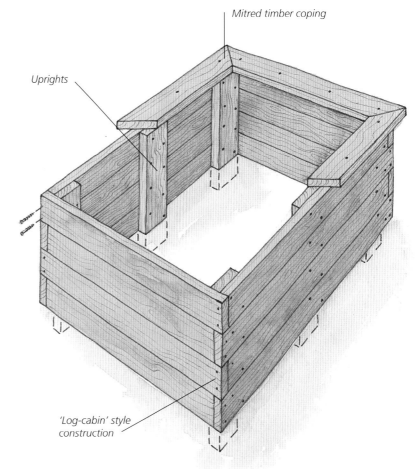

Mitred timber coping

Uprights

'Log-cabin' style construction

4

Sit all your frames on top of each other to get up to the selected height. You now need some uprights to secure them in place. Cut four more pieces of 150 x 50mm (6 x 2in) timber 10cm (4in) longer than the height of the bed. Tuck these up against the inside of each corner, one end resting at ground level, and then screw-fix to each frame from both inside and out. Each of the uprights will now be protruding about 10cm (4in) above the bed. These will become the feet. If your design has sides longer than 1.5m (5ft) you'll need more uprights half-way along each of the long sides (see **C**).Turn your frame upside-down so that the feet of the bed are standing on the ground.

5

To finish off the top of the bed, cut lengths of your tanalized 150 x 50mm (6 x 2in) timber that are 10 cm (4in) longer than the outside length and width of your bed so that they overhang the frame by 5 cm (2in) all the way around. Once they are cut, mark and saw a 45-degree line from one corner at each end (see **D**) to give you a neat mitre where the corners meet. Loose-lay the planks accurately in place (you could pin one length in place to hold it firm), then screw them together through the mitres to make the frame square and secure. Fully fix the surround down on to the top of the timber bed with screws about every 30cm (12in).

6

Once the construction is complete, add a couple of coats of paint or timber preservative. Next, decide on the position of the bed and dig holes for the feet. When it's dry, drop it into position and fill with soil.

Timber woodshed

Now, I realize that in a world of microwaves and radiators not everybody is what you'd call desperate for a woodshed nowadays. However, for those of you who do have the odd log that needs a new home, or even for those of you who just have a load of garden junk you want to hide, this is a quick and stylish way to knock up a pretty substantial timber shelter.

TIME

1 day

COST

approx. £85.00 for a 3 x 1m
(10 x 4ft) shed

TOOLS

Spade and shovel

Saw, hammer and paintbrush

Screwdriver and drill

Spirit level and square

MATERIALS

Tanalized timber, 150 x 50mm (6 x 2in)

Screws and pins

Tanalized timber, 50 x 50mm (2 x 2in)

Featheredge boarding

Timber batten 50 x 25mm (2 x 1in)

Ballast and cement for concrete

Exterior paint or timber preservative

1

Decide on the dimensions of your intended shed (this one is 2.5m x 60cm/8 x 2ft), and clear enough level ground to accommodate it. Using 150 x 50mm (6 x 2in) tanalized timber, measure, cut and fix together the first 'three-sided' layer. These three planks are simply secured with a couple of screws in the ends of the short sides. Drill pilot holes first. Create a second layer in exactly the same way as your first, but, log-cabin style so that alternate ends overlap at the corners. Loose-lay this on top of the first layer (see **A**).

2

Decide on your final height for the shed (allowing for the back to be 15cm/6in higher than the front) and then cut three lengths of 150 x 50mm (6 x 2in) timber so that they are exactly 15cm (6in) longer than the height at the back, and cut two lengths of 150 x 50mm (6 x 2in) so that they are exactly 15cm (6in) longer than the height at the front. Turn them so that they rest upright on the ground and position them inside their respective corners, with the third longer upright in the middle of the long back. (Note: the back of our shed had to be built on top of an existing wall, but I would normally recommend that you build your shed directly on to the ground.)

3

Use a spirit level to make sure all the uprights are vertical, then secure them in place by screwing in from the outside of the second layer (see **B** and **C**). Three screws per upright is plenty. Now, remove the first layer from underneath and bring it up to sit on top of the second layer. Secure it in place by screwing through to the five uprights. You have now created the first two layers of your shed, with the uprights projecting 15cm (6in) downwards to allow for burying them in post holes in the ground. You can already afford to feel pretty pleased with yourself at this stage, but it's still too early to be cocky…

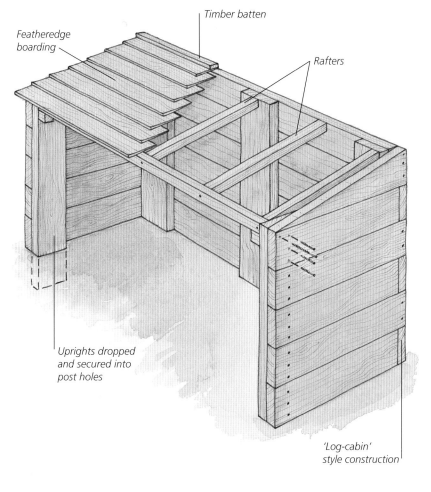

Timber batten

Featheredge boarding

Rafters

Uprights dropped and secured into post holes

'Log-cabin' style construction

4

Continue to build and secure the subsequent layers of your shed log-cabin style until you complete the last one. The height should exactly match the height of your three uprights at the front. If it doesn't, please refer to the first part of Step 2, and don't call me. Now, to create the sloping sides that complete the tops of the walls, take one piece of 150 x 50mm (6 x 2in) timber cut to the length of the sides and split it diagonally to give you two sloping triangles. Secure these to the two uprights in the front corners and also put a couple of screws down into the walls below, towards the back. That's the sides complete – now all you need is a roof.

5

Using 50 x 50mm (2 x 2in) tanalized timber, cut a length that will fit across the front and between the top corners of your two front uprights. Screw right through the walls and uprights into each end of this front rail, to fix it in place. You can make the rail even more secure by screwing in some little blocks of 50 x 50mm (2 x 2in) timber under each end for additional support.

6

Cut an overlong length of 50 x 50mm (2 x 2in) timber to create your first rafter. Rest it in place so that it spans the back wall and the front rail,

then mark the vertical lines which correspond to the inside face of both the back wall and the front rail. Cut this rafter to size and use it as a template for the others. You'll need rafters about every 45cm (18in) along the width of the shed. Fix all your rafters into place (so they are flush with the top of the back wall and the top of the front rail) by screwing straight into each end (see **D**).

7

Using featheredge boarding and working from the front of the shed to the back, complete the roof by pinning these slats into place. Each featheredge board should overlap the previous one by about 5cm (2in), and you should aim to have the whole roof overlap the shed by about 5cm (2in) on both sides and at the back (see **E**). Finally, screw down a long 50 x 25mm (2 x 1in) batten, placed on the roof exactly above the width of the back wall.

8

Now, using the marks your five uprights have already made in the ground as a guide, dig out 15cm (6in) post holes and drop your finished shed back into place. Depending on the activity of local wind or woodshed thieves, pack the post holes out with soil or concrete (6 parts ballast to 1 part cement) – see page 26. Add exterior paint or a timber preservative.

Timber garden table

This has to be one of my favourite projects in the whole book. Not only is this table great fun to make, not only does this table withstand some serious use when it's complete, not only does this table look very impressive stood out in the garden – but you can actually eat off the thing as well.

TIME
1 day

COST
approx. £50.00 for a table
2 x 1m (8 x 4ft)

TOOLS
Hammer and saw
Screwdriver
Spirit level, square and clamp
Drill
Paintbrush

MATERIALS
Tanalized timber, 100 x 100mm
(4 x 4in), for the legs
Tanalized timber, 150 x 25mm
(6 x 1in)
Exterior wood glue
Screws

1

The actual dimensions of the table are up to you, but if you want to fit normal chairs around it the first thing you're going to need are four 75cm (30in) lengths of 100 x 100mm (4 x 4in) tanalized timber to make the legs. The 'rails' that will join these legs around the top are made from 150 x 25mm (6 x 1in) tanalized timber and should be cut 10cm (4in) shorter than the eventual length and width of the finished table top. You'll need two side rails to run the length of your table and seven cross rails to span the width.

2

Lay one of your short cross rails about 15cm (6in) from the bottom of two table legs, push the legs out to the very ends of the rail, make sure everything is square, and then secure into place with an exterior wood glue and three screws into each leg. Make this end frame secure by fixing a second cross rail to the top of the other side of the legs. Use more glue and another three screws into each leg (see **A**). Use the other two legs and another two cross rails to make a second end frame identical to the first.

3

Stand the end frames up on end so that the two cross rails that are 15cm (6in) in from the bottom are on the ground and facing towards

each other. Take your two long side rails and clamp them into position spanning the two end frames, one on either side. The ends of these side rails should be flush with the outer face of the cross rails at the top of the legs (see **B**).

4

Make sure everything is straight and true with a spirit level, then check it all again. Once you're sure it's all straight, screw the side rails on to the legs to secure them in place.

5

Turn the table on its back, take one of the three cross rails and place it between the side rails, in the middle of the table. Glue and fix it into position by screwing through the side rails and into the ends of the cross rail (see **C**).

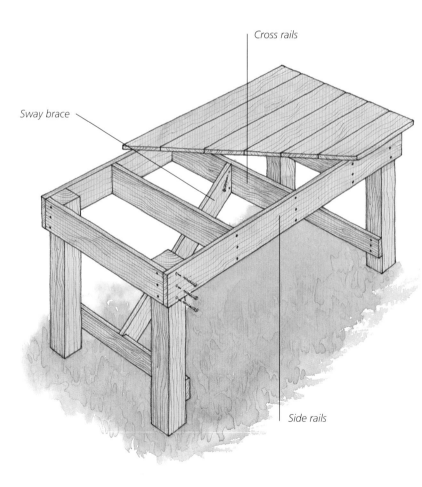

Cross rails

Sway brace

Side rails

FURNITURE AND FEATURES

6

Now turn your table back the right way up and measure up from the lower cross rails (towards the bottom of the legs) to the centre cross rail (which you have just secured in the middle of the table). Use some more 150 x 25mm (6 x 1in) timber to cut overlong 'sway braces' which will eventually span this diagonal. Clamp the first overlong sway brace in position against the side of the table. It should be level with the top of the centre cross rail at one end and about 2.5cm (1in) above the top of the lower cross where it meets the legs (see **D**). Once it's lined up and firmly clamped, mark some cutting lines at each end of the sway brace. At the top end you need to mark a vertical line down that matches the face of the centre cross rail, while at the bottom you need to mark out what's called a 'birdsmouth'. This allows

most of the sway brace's end to press flush against the lower cross rail, but also allows the very top of it to hook over the cross rail and rest on top.

7

Once it's marked up, remove the sway brace and saw along the cut lines. If you're confident that your table is perfectly symmetrical, use this sway brace as a template to cut one for the other side. If not, repeat Step 6. Fix both these pieces into place with more glue and screws driven in at an angle through the sway brace and into the cross rails. Next, glue and fix the final two cross rails into place, so that they are evenly spaced on either side of the central cross rail (see **E**).

8

Cut more lengths of 150 x 25mm (6 x 1in) tanalized timber to create the planking for the table top. You want

to leave this top overhanging the rails below by about 5cm (2in) at each end and 2.5cm (1in) at the sides. Make sure the planks are evenly spaced across the top of the table (you should consider this when calculating the initial width of your table) and screw them down on to the rails (see **F**). All the planks should be butted right up close to each other, but this will give you some problems when the weather turns wet and the timber starts to swell. A lazy way to deal with this is to lay the planks so that the curve of the end grain is the opposite way up for each neighbouring plank. The professional way is to drill two small holes where you will place fixing screws and use a small file to join them into oval openings. Then put the screws through the centre of the openings. The holes allow the wood to swell and shrink without pulling on the screws and warping the wood.

Timber window box

When you've finally run out of areas to build on or bury in the garden, there's only one thing for it: turn to the house. All houses need windows and most windows could cope with a window box or two, so here's a very quick trick to creating some rugged containers, custom-made to suit any sill.

TIME
2 hours

COST
approx. £4.00

TOOLS
Saw and square
Drill and screwdriver
Paintbrush

MATERIALS
Tanalized timber, 150 x 25mm (6 x 1in)
Tanalized timber, 50 x 25mm (2 x 1in)
Exterior wood glue
Screws
Exterior paint or timber preservative

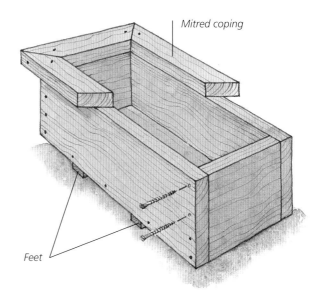

Mitred coping

Feet

1

Measure your windowsill and aim to create a box that is at least 5cm (2in) smaller at each end. From a plank of tanalized 150 x 25mm (6 x 1in) timber, cut off two pieces that match the intended length of your finished window box, one that is 50mm (2in) shorter than this, to form the base and then two 150mm (6in) lengths to form the ends.

2

Using an exterior wood glue and securing screws, fix one long length to each outside edge of the base to create an open ended trough, the base of which is 25mm (1in) shorter than the sides, at each end (see **A**). Then glue and screw in the two end pieces to make the box shape complete (see **B**).

3

From a length of 50 x 25mm (2 x 1in) tanalized timber, cut two pieces 20cm (8in) long and two pieces 5cm (2in) longer than the outside length of your window box. Draw and saw a 45–degree angle at each end of these four pieces and then lay them flat around the top edge of the box so that they are flush with the inside edge and neatly mitred at the corners. Glue and screw down into place, with one screw fixed into the end of each mitre to hold the corners tight (see **C**).

4

Turn the box over and add two more lengths of 50 x 25mm (2 x 1in) timber underneath. Cut these about 5cm (2in) shorter than the width of the box and then glue and screw them into place so that they are

2.5cm (1in) away from the edges and ends. While you have the box at your mercy in this position, you might as well drill a few drainage holes in the bottom.

5

Add a coat of exterior paint or some timber preservative, let everything dry overnight, and get planting. By the way, whatever paint or preservative you decide to use, make sure it's a water-based one so that your plants don't suffer any adverse chemical reactions. Not everyone wants genetically modified marigolds outside their window…

Obelisk climber

This climber project is constructed with a fairly straightforward 'ladder frame' technique. Once you've got the hang of it, it's easy to see how it could apply to other constructions in the garden. You can either build the obelisk as I have described here, or you can just take the fundamental principles and use them on a far more elaborate design of your own.

1

Cut four pieces of 25 x 25mm (1 x 1in) tanalized timber to the height you want. Decide on the width and depth, and then cut cross pieces of the timber to match these. For every 30cm (12in) in height you'll need four cross pieces.

2

Lay out two uprights and space out the cross pieces between them to make an evenly spaced ladder with the top and bottom 'rungs' about 15cm (6in) in from each end and the remaining cross pieces at about 30cm (12in) gaps between them. Drill pilot holes through the uprights and into the ends of each cross piece. Use exterior wood glue and a screw to secure each joint. Leave the heads flush with the surface of the wood (see **A**). Repeat the process to create a second ladder exactly like the first.

3

Using the same pilot hole/glue/screw fixing technique, use your remaining cross pieces to join the two ladder frames together. These new cross pieces go in at exactly the same height as the existing 'rungs' on the ladder frames. Be careful not to let the screws meet on the way (see **B**).

4

A wooden drawer handle glued to the top of each upright finishes the whole thing off perfectly (see **C**). Paint with exterior paint or a timber preservative and leave to dry.

5

Dig little holes in the ground for the bottom of the legs to sit in. They don't need to be deep, and if you're on soft soil, and you're careful, you could even just press the obelisk into place when you position it.

Wooden drawer handles

Cross pieces

Ladder frames

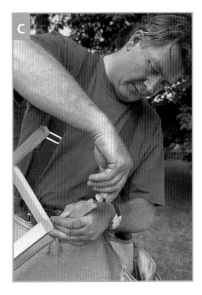

QUESTIONS and ANSWERS

If you've still got queries after reading this book, here are a few of the more common questions that you might be tempted to ask, already answered. How's that for service?

Q

I've decided to put up a new panel fence in the back garden, but I'm not sure how to stop it leaning over in the wind while the concrete around each post sets.

A

If you're at all worried about what will happen to a new fence while the concrete goes off, and particularly if you live in an area prone to high winds, here's how to keep everything upright, while your concrete goes rock hard.

Using some old scrap timber planks or some decent sized battens (minimum 50 x 25mm/2 x 1in), cut lengths of about 1.5–2 metres (5–6ft) to use as props for each of the fence posts. Ideally, you would actually put these props in place as you are erecting each post, but they can be put in afterwards if you get a sudden storm warning. If you're using wooden fence posts, simply nail one end of the prop into the post, about half-way up, and nail the other end of the prop on to a wooden stake hammered into the ground a metre or so away. Obviously, you want to make sure the post is upright when you nail the prop into place, otherwise it kind of defeats the object of the exercise.

If you're using concrete posts, you can secure the prop to the concrete with a clamp, or even with a bit of rope lashed around the post or through one of the fixing holes. The other trick with concrete posts, once the concrete has gone off enough to keep them upright on their own, is to slide all the fencing panels out for the first night after the fence goes up. Without the fencing panels to catch the breeze, there will be a lot less for the wind to get hold of and push over.

A rockery makes a great focal point in a garden. Try to get hold of local stone, if possible, for a more natural look.

Q

I want to build some small retaining walls in my garden and was thinking of using railway sleepers for the job. How do I get hold of them and what should I look out for when buying some?

A

Railway sleepers are actually dead useful in the garden. They're small enough for a couple of consenting adults to manhandle them into place, but they're heavy enough to stay put and hold back a lot of soil once in position – especially if you drill holes through the ends of the sleepers and hammer steel rods through into the ground. As the railways of the world gradually replace all their old timber sleepers with the new concrete ones, you'll find these lumps of wood more and more accessible. You can start hunting at garden centres, if you're happy to pay their mark-up, but you might be better advised phoning up local timber merchants to see if they stock them. Failing that, check out your nearest architectural salvage yard for possibly the best bargains of all. Wherever they come from, there are a couple of different types to look out for.

Firstly, sleepers come in softwood or hardwood. The softwood ones are lighter and cheaper, but the heavier and more expensive hardwood varieties might actually be more suitable for retaining-wall duties. Sleepers in Britain are usually crammed full of a very sticky tar-based preservative, which can melt and seep out in the summer. Shop around and you may be able to find sleepers that are imported from places like Scandinavia, where the preservative treatment is much more like a tanalizing process and leaves nothing to drip off when the heat is on.

Q

I'd like to build a rockery out of natural stone, but have no idea where to find some.

A

Well, at the risk of stating the obvious, the first place to look is in the telephone directory under 'stone merchants'. Ring round a few numbers and get an idea of what's available and how much it's going to cost. You can also go to some of the larger DIY sheds or garden centres nowadays, but you will inevitably end up paying them a premium for putting the rocks in neat little bags or stacking them on a pretty wooden pallet. For the best bargains of all, go direct to the quarry. The telephone directory is a good place to start to find one of them. The other advantage of buying your stone from a local quarry is that you are guaranteed to end up with genuinely local stone. Believe me, if you are planning some major garden construction with these rocks, your best bet for everything to blend in and look like it belongs is to buy the stuff that really does.

Q

I'd like to lay a new drive, but there's an old concrete monstrosity I need to get rid of first. Where do I start?

A

Now don't get me wrong, poured concrete can look really nice as a final surface – as long as it's laid and finished properly. Unfortunately, poured concrete can also look awful, especially when it's slapped on as the quickest and cheapest option to a hard-landscaping problem. If you need to get rid of some, your best hope is that it wasn't me that put it there in the first place. When I lay concrete, it's there to stay, but not everyone is quite so fastidious about their technique…

The first thing to do is dig a little hole where the concrete ends – this will tell you how far it goes down. It will probably be only a couple of inches, but if the concrete turns out to be the roof of an old air-raid shelter you'd better start revising your plans. If it's just a layer of fairly thin concrete the first thing to do is lever it up clear of any foundations underneath. For all its apparent strength, concrete is a bit like a sheet of ice floating on the top of a pond. Flat down, you can put all the weight on it you like, but lift it up at an angle and it will shatter at the first heavy blow. So if you use some bricks and scaffold poles to lift one end of your unwanted slab of concrete a few inches up into the air, and then give it one good central whack with a sledgehammer, you could suddenly be dealing with

rubble. However, if the concrete slab is too big, or just too thick for this, there's nothing for it but to hire a 'concrete breaker' and smash it the hard way.

Finally, let me just remind you: whenever you're laying new hard surfaces that adjoin the house, always make sure you go down far enough with your clearances and/or foundation. When you build back up again your new top surface must be at least 15cm (6in) below the existing damp-proof course. Whatever it takes in terms of time or energy to achieve this, it will always, always be a lot cheaper than treating the damp or rot that might arise if you don't.

Q

I have a fairly small garden, but a fairly large family – all of whom seem to generate a terrifying amount of washing. How can I fit a decent-sized washing line that disappears when I don't want it, but isn't one of those dreadful rotary 'whirligig' contraptions, into my garden?

A

I know just what you mean. Those whirligigs drive me mad as well. Not only are they a recipe for taking your eye out in an enclosed space, I'm sure there must be all manner of creepy-crawlies living in those tubular metal arms. For my money, the best solution is one of those spring-loaded self-recoiling systems that you can buy in all the big shops nowadays. Find a good strong fixing point for the reel box itself – on a wall is ideal – and then screw it firmly into position. Now unwind the line to its full extent and see how many cleverly located cup hooks you can screw into the trees, the fences and the gateposts all around you. With a bit of careful planning you can create a neat little network of hooks that will take the extendable line in a crisscross right around the garden. Come washing day, this should give you all the hanging space you need for the family's debris. Come the weekend, the whole thing will snap back into its housing as if it had never been there.

Q

We've recently moved into a fairly old house. While the fences seem in good condition, the gate at the end of the front path is sagging badly and dragging on the ground as it swings. The construction of the gate matches the fence, so I don't want to replace it. Can I fix the gate as is?

A

A sagging gate is the result of one of two problems, or a combination of both. Either the post on to which the gate is hinged has tilted inwards, or the construction of the gate has become so old that it can't support itself any more. The first thing to do is to cut some wooden blocks that will sit under the gate to hold the whole thing up exactly where you would like it. As you lift the gate to insert these supports, notice if it is the gatepost that tilts back into place, or the joints on the gate itself that move. If the post moves, you will need to dig out the surrounding soil, to about 15cm (6in), and pack the

hole with concrete or ready-to-use powder. Don't take the supports out from under the gate until this new concrete has cured for a couple of days.

If it's the construction of the gate itself that has come loose, you need to tighten all the screws you can find, and then add a few more right through the major mortise and tenon joints which are holding most of the weight. If the holes into which existing screws go are worn and wide, it may be worth removing the screws, packing the screw-holes with a bit of dowelling (or just some matchsticks), and then popping new screws back in. Failing all that, you can now get a wide selection of galvanized steel brackets to reinforce the corners and joints that form your gate. Screw these into place wherever the above tactics prove ineffective and you should end up with a gate that's every bit as perky as the day it first became a swinger.

If you want to block off a bit of the garden, but don't want to obscure the view, a post-and-rail fence is an unobtrusive option.

Q

There's an old brick wall at the end of my garden that I would dearly love to keep. However, the bricks and mortar are showing bad signs of weathering and the whole wall has a crack at one end. Do I need to demolish it and start again?

A

You see so little nice brickwork around modern houses these days that I'm always very unwilling to say goodbye to any old wall if there's a chance of saving it. The first thing you need to do is assess the damage. Weathering of the mortar between the bricks is just a fact of life, I'm afraid, but hardly serious. Erosion of the bricks themselves can also be common on the weather side of the wall, where damp can get blown into the very fabric of the bricks and then freeze solid, forcing off bits of the brick's surface as it does so. This is more serious than the decaying mortar, but still far from terminal.

Cracks down the wall usually come in two varieties. Those that follow the line of the joins usually signify nothing worse than a bit of shoddy mortar mixing when the wall was first built. Cracks that cut vertically down through the bricks themselves are indicative of something rather more serious, like the S word: subsidence. Weathered or cracked mortar can be raked out with a screwdriver, or a cold chisel and hammer. Once you're back to where the mortar becomes firm again you can use the point of a trowel to push in some new mortar to repoint the affected area. Thoroughly wash and wet the brickwork before you do this as it will take the mortar far better that way. It all becomes fairly straightforward, once you've got the hang of it.

Ironically, the hardest thing is actually getting the new mortar to match the colour of the old, so you may want to experiment with colouring agents. Remember, mortar never takes on its true colour until it's dry. Just before the new mortar is dry, you should finish off the pointing in the style which matches the rest of the wall.

Walls with mellowed bricks add a feeling of maturity to a garden. If you can possibly preserve them it's always worth the trouble.

When the surface of the bricks themselves has come away, there are two routes you can go. The most laborious option is to chip out all the mortar surrounding the affected brick and then slot in a new brick of a matching colour, using your repointing skills to secure it. On the other hand, the easy way is to wash and clean all the offending bricks and then slap on some special water-repellent solution to keep any new moisture out, from here on in. You will still be left with a surface that some might refer to as 'knackered', but you should simply describe it as 'rustic'.

Cracks that run right down through the actual bricks in the wall are not so easy to dismiss. If the crack is still slowly opening (check with bits of string glued across the gap) you have a subsidence problem and there is little choice other than to demolish the wall, rebuild the foundations, and start again. However, if the crack isn't opening (and doesn't for a good six months), then you're probably safe to repoint in the normal way.

Q

I love cooking outdoors and want to build a permanent brick barbecue. What should I do?

A

OK, you have hit upon both aspects of the problem right there in the question. You like cooking, and you want a permanent barbecue. Some would say the two are mutually exclusive. Let's deal with the 'permanent' side first. Permanent means you're not going to be moving this construction once it's built, so you need to be absolutely sure it's in the right place when you build it. For instance… Does it catch enough breeze to keep the coals hot? Is it sheltered enough to keep the food warm? Is it near enough to where the party will be to keep you involved? Is it far enough away from the party to keep all your guests out of the smoke? The only way to be sure that these issues are addressed is to spend one whole summer with a portable barbecue. Once you're happy with a location for this, you can be fairly sure that will be the best place to build your permanent replacement.

To build the thing out of brick is really not as hard as you might think. Make sure that you're on solid foundations – the patio is fine, or a little pad of concrete poured on the soil – and then use the techniques I describe for building a brick wall on page 36. The trick is to take your time and make sure every course is straight and level before you move up.

Now, you like cooking. If you really do like cooking, the last thing you're going to want to work with is some single-height, single-heat, inflexible monstrosity that burns everything when it's first lit and then induces a variety of undercooked food poisoning issues as it cools. A good barbecue for a good cook needs some variety in the height at which your grill can rest. However you design the finished thing, make sure you incorporate a system whereby there are at least three different levels at which to secure the grill. You may not think it's worth the extra aggravation, but your dinner guests certainly will.

A deck makes a wonderful area for entertaining friends on summer evenings.

Stockists and Suppliers

BUILDING SUPPLIERS

Graham Group plc
(Head Office)
96 Leeds Road
Huddersfield HD1 4RH
Tel. 01484 537366

Jewson Group
Sutherland House
Matlock Road
Foles Hill
Coventry CV1 4JQ
Tel. 01203 669100
Customer tel. 0800 539766

Lazdans
(reclaimed building materials)
218 Bow Common Lane
Bow
London E3 4HH
Tel: 0181 981 4632

Travis Perkins
Lodge Way House
Harlestone Road
Northampton NN5 7UG
Tel. 01604 752424

PAVING

Atlas Copco Construction and
Mining (concrete breaker)
PO Box 79
Swallowdale Lane
Hemel Hempstead
Hertfordshire HP2 7HA
Tel. 01442 222414

Marshalls (Heritage Yorkstone
Circle Paving)
Southowram
Halifax HX3 9SY
Tel. 01422 306300

Park Products Ltd (slab lifter)
Green Bank Technology Park
Challenge Way
Blackburn BB1 5QJ
Tel. 01254 614004

Stonemarket Concrete Ltd
(millstone paving)
Old Gravel Quarry
Oxford Road
Ryton-on-Dunsmore
Warwickshire CV8 3EJ
Tel. 01203 305530

Town and Country Paving Ltd
(paving, bricks etc)
Unit 10
Shrublands Nurseries
Roundstone Lane
Angering
Littlehampton
West Sussex BN16 4AT
Tel. 01903 776297

POWER TOOLS

Black and Decker
210 Bath Road
Slough
Berkshire SL1 3YD
Tel. 01753 574277

Bosch
PO Box 98
Uxbridge
Middlesex UB9 5HJ
Tel. 01895 838791

DeWalt
210 Bath Road
Slough
Berkshire SL1 3YD
Tel. 01753 567055

Greenbrook Electrical plc
(powerbreaker RCDs)
7 Astra Centre
Edinburgh Way
Harlow
Essex CM20 2BG
Tel. 01279 434561

Paslode (Division of ITW)
(impulse cordless nailers)
Queensway
Fforestfach
Swansea SA5 4ED
Tel. 01792 589800

Sandvik Saws and Tools UK
Manor Way
Halesowen
West Midlands B62 8QZ
Tel. 0121 504 5200

TIMBER

T Chamber and Son Ltd
(tanalized timber)
70/72 Leyton Road
Stratford
London E15 1DG
Tel. 0181 534 6318

Cuprinol Paints (timber stains
and preservatives)
Cuprinol Ltd
Adderwell
Frome
Somerset BA11 1NL
Tel. 01373 475000
Fax. 01373 475010

Dandf Design
(kit arbour, decking)
Hillcroft Works
Carleton Road
Pontefract WF8 3RW
Tel. 01977 704796

Forest Fencing plc
(trellises, posts, fence panels)
Stanford Court
Stanford Bridge
Nr Worcester WR6 6SR
Tel.01886 812451

H S Jackson & Son (Fencing) Ltd
(machine-rounded posts)
Stowting Common
Ashford
Kent TN25 6BN
Tel. 01233 750393

Jimmy's Joinery (purpose-
made timber structures)
1 Warner Place
London E2 7DA
Tel: 0171 739 6407

Rusticraft (rustic arbours,
trellises and furniture)
312A Brant Road
Lincoln LN5 9AF
Tel. 01522 721014

TURF

Hollingsworth Turfs
Nagshead Lane
Brentwood
Essex
Tel. 01277 211614

Rolawn Ltd
Elvington
York YO41 4XR
Tel. 01904 608661

Sean Allen
(turf stripping machine)
7 Lampole
Station Road
Overton
Hampshire RG25 3TL
Tel. 01256 773165

Index

PICTURE CREDITS

BBC Worldwide would like to thank the following for providing photographs and for
permission to reproduce copyright material. While every effort has been made to
trace and acknowledge all copyright holders, we would like to apologize should
there be any errors or omissions.

Garden Matters 47b, 124; The Garden Picture Library 30, 34, 35, 36, 39, 40, 76, 90l,
90r, 91, 92; John Glover 93, 121; Photos Horticultural 31; Jo Whitworth 94.
All other photographs © BBC Worldwide Ltd/Susan Bell.